HOW TO DIAGRAM ANY SENTENCE

Exercises to Accompany
The Diagramming Dictionary

HOW TO DIAGRAM ANY SENTENCE

Exercises to Accompany
The Diagramming Dictionary

BY JESSICA OTTO AND SUSAN WISE BAUER

DIAGRAMS BY PATTY REBNE

WELL-
TRAINED
MIND
PRESS

Names: Bauer, Susan Wise, author. | Otto, Jessica, author. | Rebne, Patty, illustrator. | Otto, Jessica. Diagramming dictionary.
Title: How to diagram any sentence : exercises to accompany The diagramming dictionary / Susan Wise Bauer and Jessica Otto ; diagrams by Patty Rebne.
Description: Charles City, Virginia : Well-Trained Mind Press, [2022] | Interest age level: 13 and up. | Summary: Diagramming a sentence shows you how it is (or isn't) working, and unlocks the door to clear, balanced writing. These exercises by grammar experts Susan Wise Bauer and Jessica Otto use sentences by classic and contemporary authors to give students practice in every diagramming rule covered in The Diagramming Dictionary, from the simplest noun-verb sentences to challenging, complex pieces from Dickens and Austen. Full answers are provided at the back of the book.--Publisher.
Identifiers: ISBN: 978-1-952469-35-0 (paperback) | 978-1-952469-39-8 (ebook) | LCCN: 2022945061
Subjects: LCSH: English language--Grammar--Problems, exercises, etc.-- Juvenile literature. | English language--Sentences--Problems, exercises, etc.--Juvenile literature. | English language-- Rhetoric--Problems, exercises, etc.-- Juvenile literature. | CYAC: English language--Grammar-- Problems, exercises, etc. | English language--Sentences--Problems, exercises, etc. | English language--Rhetoric--Problems, exercises, etc. | LCGFT: Problems and exercises.
Classification: LCC: LB1631 .B382 2022 | DDC: 428.00712--dc23

1 2 3 4 5 6 7 8 9 10 MER 30 29 28 27 26 25 24 23 22
HtDAS-0922

TABLE OF CONTENTS

HOW TO USE THIS BOOK

How to Diagram Any Sentence gives you the opportunity to practice hands-on diagramming, based on the principles in *The Diagramming Dictionary*. Reading through *The Diagramming Dictionary* will tell you *how* to diagram, but working through the exercises in this book will make that knowledge real. (As you already know, you remember some of what you read—but much more of what you *do*.)

Start out by reading the Foreword in *The Diagramming Dictionary*. That will provide you with the rationale behind diagramming (why should you bother?), along with plenty of practical suggestions for your own diagramming practice.

Then, have a quick look through the next short section of *The Diagramming Dictionary*, Before We Begin, to make sure that you understand the basis of all diagrams (the subject/predicate division).

And you're ready to go.

How to Diagram Any Sentence follows the exact same progression as *The Diagramming Dictionary*. So read through the rule in the *Dictionary*, look at the sample diagram, and then turn to *How to Diagram* to complete the exercises. Then, check your work.

For example: The first section in Part I of the *Dictionary* is IA, Simple subjects. And the first simple subject (IA.1) is common nouns: "When a common noun is used as the subject of a sentence, put it on the subject line." Read the definition, examine the diagram, and then turn to *How to Diagram Any Sentence*. You'll see the exact same first section (IA, Simple subjects) and then the first exercise—four sentences with common nouns as subjects. Modelling your work on the example in the *Dictionary*, diagram the subject and predicate of each sentence. Then, check your work against the Answer Key in the second half of the book.

That's all there is to it! You can move on to IA.2 (the understood you as subject), and then IA.3 (pronouns as subjects), always checking the definition and example in the *Dictionary* first, and then putting that knowledge to use by diagramming the exercises in *How to Diagram*.

A few things to keep in mind:

Because every sentence has a subject and a predicate, it's impossible to do even a basic diagram without putting both of those parts of the sentence on your sketch. So until you learn about predicates in Section IB, the predicate of each sentence will be underlined for you. Don't worry about what's underlined. Just put it in the predicate space. (That's why you needed to read Before We Begin, so if you skipped that part of the instructions above, go back and look at it now.)

So that you can learn one diagramming concept at a time, *How to Diagram* puts sentence parts that you haven't yet learned in italics. Only diagram the words in regular type, and don't worry about the rest. Sometimes we have included the entire sentence diagram in the Key, just for your own interest.

And finally: Whenever possible, we've drawn the sentences in the exercises from the books of actual accomplished writers and indicated this with a footnote. If there's no footnote, the sentence was invented in order to illustrate a particular grammatical rule.

Sharpen your pencil, grab some unlined paper and an eraser, and start diagramming!

WHY DIAGRAMMING IS HELPFUL FOR ADULT WRITERS

If you feel uncertain about the clarity of your written sentences—and who hasn't?—sentence diagramming can help you crack the mysterious code of the English language.

The whole point of written English is to say, as plainly as possible, exactly what you mean. And although that sounds simple, hundreds of thousands of intelligent and talented grown-ups managed to get through twelve years of primary and secondary school without being given the tools needed for this task. Many of them also earned college degrees, and even graduate degrees, and still find themselves struggling to write effective sentences.

Diagramming can show you why a sentence is, or isn't, working—with a minimum of wasted time. Diagrams are a simple, visual representation of the logical relationship between the words in a sentence. If those words have a clear relationship to each other, you'll get your point across.

Think of diagramming as a wellness check on your sentences. A thought begins in your brain as a wordless idea; you put that idea into words; and then you put those words down on paper. Often, there's a disconnect between the second and third steps. When we talk to each other, we rely on nonverbal cues: tone of voice, physical gestures, pauses, and accents. But if you need to convey that same idea to someone who's not in the room with you, you can't rely on any of those useful aids. You've got to make every word in your written sentence count.

And too often, written sentences are incomplete, bloated, incoherent, or rambling.

How do you know if you're communicating clearly? Put the sentence you're struggling with on a diagram. If you can't figure out where a part of the sentence fits into the diagram, you're probably dealing with a thought that doesn't belong. If the diagram doesn't make sense, neither does your sentence. (And the reader won't get the idea either.)

But if you can put your sentence on a diagram with confidence? You can be sure that you've had your say with as much clarity as possible.

WHY DIAGRAMMING IS HELPFUL FOR STUDENT LEARNERS

Imagine that you are sitting at a small table covered with Lego pieces of every kind: square ones, rounded sections, long bricks, and those flat rectangles that are so annoying to take apart. By themselves, these plastic blocks are not very useful. You could look at each one individually and identify its shape and color, but until you pick the pieces up and start connecting them, all you will have is a pile of bricks.

When students learn the parts of a sentence, they are collecting their own grammar pieces. They memorize, for example, that a direct object answers the question "who?" or "what?" and receives the action of a verb. They learn that a predicate nominative follows a linking verb and renames a subject. But they don't always learn how those parts work together, and diagramming sentences is one of the best tools we have to show students how to connect these pieces and construct a good sentence.

Let's say that a student adds a prepositional phrase to a sentence, in order to give some nice detail and add description. If a student has practiced diagramming, she will know, from seeing how the lines of the diagram connect, what word this prepositional phrase is modifying. If that phrase is acting as an adjective, the placement in the sentence becomes even more important. Here's an example from *Grammar for the Well-Trained Mind*:

Inside the clock, Daniel watched the huge, swinging pendulum.

In this sentence, the prepositional phrase "Inside the clock" is in the wrong spot. Diagramming this phrase forces a student to make a decision: Is this phrase acting as an adjective or adverb? Does it belong under (modify) the word "watched" or something else? Is the pendulum inside the clock or is Daniel? Once a student recognizes this phrase as adjectival, she would then realize that the phrase is a misplaced modifier, and that it needs to be put directly after the noun "pendulum."

Diagramming sentences creates a visual representation for the student of how the sentence parts she has studied all click together. It gives younger students a chance to try out some critical thinking skills and learn a bit of analysis, and it allows more experienced students to see how various types of clauses and structures all work together to create a lovely-sounding group of words, much like how that jumbled pile of Lego bricks can, once connected, become something to enjoy.

It is our hope that, if you have never diagrammed before, this book will introduce you to a new, useful tool for you and your students as you craft your phrases and clauses and paragraphs. Happy diagramming!

PART I: HOW TO DIAGRAM THE SIMPLE SUBJECT AND SIMPLE PREDICATE OF A SENTENCE

IA. Simple subjects

1. Common nouns as subjects

   1. Meteorologists <u>issue</u> *hurricane warnings.*

   2. *The enormous* elephant <u>entered</u> *the elevator.*

   3. *A heartbroken* hedgehog <u>hijacked</u> *the helicopter*!

   4. *A light* rain <u>fell</u> *in the morning.*

2. The understood you as subject

   1. <u>Learn</u> *quietly.*

   2. <u>Eat</u> *your vegetables*!

   3. <u>Mail</u> *the letter.*

   4. <u>Close</u> *the oven.*

3. Pronouns as subjects

   1. <u>Are</u> you *hungry?*

   2. I <u>see</u> *a mouse!*

   3. He <u>stood</u> *bravely at the fortress door.*[1]

   4. I <u>mowed</u> *the grass.*

4. Compound nouns as subjects

   1. *Early* trout fishing <u>succeeds</u>.

   2. *Kristi's* ice cream <u>melted</u>.

   3. *Our* solar system <u>moves</u>.

   4. *Sydney's* fishtank <u>bubbled</u>.

---

1. *The Phantom Tollbooth*, Norton Juster

5. Compound subjects

    1. *The* Rainbow's Daughter and *the* Rose Princess <u>approached</u> *them*.[2]

    2. Alexandra and Raphael <u>play</u> *tic-tac-toe together*.

    3. Water and nutrients <u>are</u> *sufficient for the cultivation of tomatoes*.[3]

    4. *The* confusion and clangor <u>lasted</u> *a few seconds*.[4]

6. Compound subjects with more than one coordinating conjunction

    1. *A* plate and *a* cup and *a* fork <u>sat</u> *on the counter*.

    2. Cheeseburgers or hot dogs or bratwurst <u>are</u> *the choices for the picnic*.

    3. *The* dog and *the* cat and *the new* puppy <u>lay</u> *on the porch*.

    4. <u>Are</u> pillows and blankets and towels *in the basket?*

7. Proper nouns as subjects

    1. Juliana <u>recycles</u>.

    2. Marie Curie <u>researched</u>.

    3. Louisa May Alcott <u>wrote</u>.

    4. *The homemade* Flying Machine <u>disappeared</u>.[5]

8. Indefinite pronouns as subjects

    1. Nobody <u>knows</u> *him*.[6]

    2. Something <u>did happen</u>.[7]

    3. Nothing <u>came</u> *of the move*.[8]

    4. Few <u>are</u> *angels*.[9]

---

2. *Tik-Tok of Oz*, L. Frank Baum
3. *Plants, Algae, and Fungi*, Britannica Illustrated Science Library
4. *Maese Perez, the Organist*, Gustavo Adolfo Bequer
5. *The Magical Land of Noom*, Johnny Gruelle
6. *Oliver Twist*, Charles Dickens
7. *The Borrowers*, Mary Norton
8. *The Knights Hospitaller: A Military History of the Knights of St. John*, John C. Carr
9. *King Henry the Eighth*, William Shakespeare

9. Prepositional phrases as subjects

> If you do not know how to diagram a prepositional phrase, please see section IIIA 1 in *The Diagramming Dictionary*.
>   If you do not know how to diagram a prepositional phrase as a subject, please see section IIIB 1 in *The Diagramming Dictionary*.

1. Before breakfast <u>is</u> *too early.*

2. In *the* sun <u>is</u> *too hot today.*

3. In *her mother's* arms <u>is</u> *the newborn baby's favorite place.*

4. During *the* class <u>is</u> *a bad time for a nap.*

10. Demonstrative pronouns as subjects

1. This <u>smells</u> *funny.*

2. This <u>was</u> *a further indication of the truth.*[10]

3. *In text-only games,* this <u>is</u> *the only description available.*[11]

4. That <u>is</u> *a most unjust accusation.*[12]

11. Interrogative pronouns as subjects

1. Who <u>brought</u> *this?*

2. Who <u>spilled</u> *this Smoking Bishop punch on the floor?*

3. Which <u>is</u> *the best fish market in Tokyo?*

4. Whose <u>is</u> *that beautiful garden?*

12. Contractions as subjects

1. We'll <u>play</u> *bandits, or forts, or soldiers, or any of the old games.*[13]

2. You'<u>re</u> *not* <u>making</u> *that fuss about one old wolf?*[14]

3. It'<u>s</u> *the only book for all surfers.*[15]

4. He'<u>s</u> *unbeatable* and <u>drops</u> *the dehuller with a fat Yes.*[16]

---

10. *The Histories* by Herodotus (translation by Aubrey de Sélincourt)
11. *What is Your Quest?: From Adventure Games to Interactive Books*, Anastasia Salter
12. *The Devil to Pay,* Dorothy Sayers
13. *Five Children and It,* E. Nesbit
14. *The Witch of Blackbird Pond,* Elizabeth George Speare
15. *Barbarian Days: A Surfing Life,* William Finnegan
16. "No Face," Junot Díaz

13. Intensive pronouns with a subject

    1. *During those days, the* sonnet itself <u>exploded</u> *out of me.*[17]

    2. *Of this,* I myself <u>am</u> <u>certain</u> and <u>am</u> *fully* <u>resolved</u>.

    3. I myself <u>suffer</u> *from a different kind of education.* [18]

    4. *Before the storm, the* mayor herself <u>will describe</u> *this new evacuation plan for the city.*

14. Gerunds as subjects

    1. Loving <u>is</u> *never a waste of time.*[19]

    2. Arguing <u>will</u> *not* <u>solve</u> *your problems.*

    3. Hoping <u>propelled</u> *them forward.*

    4. Tracking <u>was</u> *painfully slow work.*[20]

15. Infinitives as subjects

    1. To stay <u>seemed</u> *the best way to her.* [21]

    2. To exist <u>is</u> *to change.*[22]

    3. To live <u>is</u> *to die.*

    4. To wish <u>was</u> *to hope.*

---

17. Claude McKay, quoted in *The Civil Rights Movement*, Elizabeth Sirimarco
18. *The Library of the World's Best Literature, Ancient and Modern*, Vol. 12, ed. Charles Dudley Warner
19. Astrid Alauda
20. *Big Red*, Jim Kjelgaard
21. *The Matchlock Gun*, Walter D. Edmonds
22. Henri Bergson

16. Compound subjects with coordinating correlative conjunctions

    1. Both *his* wife and *his* brothers <u>were delighted</u> *to see the coming of the dawn.*

    2. Neither *your* discourse nor *your* remonstrances <u>shall change</u> *my mind.*[23]

    3. Neither *the* jackal nor *the* peacock <u>was</u> *able to pass the test.*

    4. *In 424,* both *Darius II's* father and *his* half-brother <u>died</u>.[24]

17. Appositive nouns after subjects

    1. She <u>would remain</u> *detached, a* unit *in an official crowd.*[25]

    2. I, *the* man, <u>have brought</u> *here a little of the Red Flower.*[26]

    3. *Adam's* band, Shooting Star, <u>is</u> *on an upward spiral, which is a great thing—mostly.* [27]

    4. It <u>was soaring</u>, *that* voice, *warm and complicated, utterly fearless.*[28]

18. Unknown subjects with hortative verbs

    1. <u>Let</u> *the Lord of the Black Lands come forth.*[29]

    2. <u>Let</u> *the song of celebration ring out!*

    3. *The* war <u>is</u> *inevitable—and let* <u>it</u> *come!*[30]

    4. *My fellow citizens:* <u>let</u> *no one doubt that this is a difficult and dangerous effort on which we have set out.*[31]

23. *The Arabian Nights*, edited by Kate Douglas Wiggin and Nora A. Smith
24. *The History of the Ancient World*, Susan Wise Bauer
25. *Gaudy Night*, Dorothy Sayers
26. *The Jungle Book*, Rudyard Kipling
27. *If I Stay*, Gayle Forman
28. *Bel Canto*, Ann Patchett
29. *The Return of the King*, J. R. R. Tolkien
30. "Liberty or Death!" Patrick Henry
31. "On the Cuban Missile Crisis," John F. Kennedy

1B. Simple predicates

1. Helping verbs

    1. He was swimming.[32]

    2. Oliver was talking.[33]

    3. She was thinking.[34]

    4. Squirrels will gather.[35]

2. Compound predicates

    1. Leo rang *his bell twice* and tapped *his foot impatiently.*

    2. I shut *the door* and looked.[36]

    3. Gloria and Caleb clapped *enthusiastically* and *then* stood.

    4. He took *the gold* and hid *it.*[37]

3. Compound predicates with more than one coordinating conjunction or comma

    1. Reality might disconcert *her,* bewilder *her,* hurt *her, but it would not be reality.*[38]

    2. *Subsequent* dynasties repaired and added *more canals to the network* and created *a system of irrigation and flood control.*[39]

    3. *There, without a thought,* she left *the pathway,* plunged *into a field,* and fell *on the grass.* [40]

    4. He took *a large vase,* placed *money in the bottom,* filled *it with olives,* and carried *it to his friend for safekeeping.*[41]

32. *The Light Princess and Other Fairy Stories,* George MacDonald
33. *Oliver Twist,* Charles Dickens
34. *At the Back of the North Wind,* George MacDonald
35. *Stories the Iroquois Tell Their Children,* Mabel Powers
36. *Anne of Green Gables,* L.M. Montgomery
37. "The Story of Ali Cogia, Merchant of Bagdad," traditional Arab folktale
38. *Wide Sargasso Sea,* Jean Rhys
39. *Vietnam (Cultures of the World),* Audrey Seah and Charissa M. Nair
40. *The Witch of Blackbird Pond,* Elizabeth George Speare
41. "The Story of Ali Cogia, Merchant of Bagdad," traditional Arab folktale

4. Contractions as predicates

    1. They'll arrive *today*.

    2. I've *almost* broken *my neck*.[42]

    3. We're leaving *in the morning*.

    4. *There's no* meat *for breakfast*.[43]

5. The understood helping verb

    1. *As for the ghosts*, we *ourselves* had *never* seen *nor* heard *them*.[44]

    2. Ella had watered and weeded *the garden before breakfast*.

    3. *The* water was rising and filling *the basement*.

    4. *Many* boaters will decorate *their vessels* and sail *down the canals of the city*.

6. Quasi-coordinators joining compound predicates

    1. Much *of the snow at these great heights* is evaporated rather than thawed.[45]

    2. He would walk *in a hailstorm* sooner than pay *ten dollars for a cab*.

    3. *My* friend would order *takeout* sooner than wait *for a table*.

    4. *Once forward*, he fell rather than sat *in the pilot's seat* and *immediately* began checking *readouts and gauges*.[46]

42. *Rebecca of Sunnybrook Farm*, Kate Douglas Wiggin
43. *The Story of the World, Volume 1: Ancient Times*, Susan Wise Bauer
44. *Where the Flame Trees Bloom*, Alma Flor Ada
45. *The Voyage of the Beagle*, Charles Darwin
46. *Star Wars Trilogy*, George Lucas

PART II: HOW TO DIAGRAM ADJECTIVES AND ADVERBS

IIA. Adjectives

1. Descriptive Adjectives

   1. *The* hideous, powerful sea-monster thrashed.[47]

   2. *The rabbits'* tremulous noses were sniffing.[48]

   3. Fragile eggshells can break.

   4. *A* tiny music box played.

2. Compound adjectives (single adjectives made up of more than one word)

   1. *The* magnificent chestnut-brown sea otter hissed.[49]

   2. *The* long-lasting rainstorm had ended.[50]

   3. Sixty-three left-handed men responded.

   4. *The* soft-voiced cow was eating.[51]

3. Articles

   1. The *monster's* formidable death-rattle shook.[52]

   2. A laurel-hedged walk curved.[53]

   3. An out-of-breath police officer hurried.

   4. A steady buzz-buzz grew.[54]

---

47. *Twenty Thousand Leagues Under the Sea*, Jules Verne
48. *The Secret Garden*, Frances Hodgson Burnett
49. *Twenty Thousand Leagues Under the Sea*, Jules Verne
50. *The Secret Garden*, Frances Hodgson Burnett
51. *The Magical Land of Noom*, Johnny Gruelle
52. *Twenty Thousand Leagues Under the Sea*, Jules Verne
53. *The Secret Garden,* Frances Hodgson Burnett
54. *The Magical Land of Noom*, Johnny Gruelle

4. Compound adjectives (two or more adjectives modifying the same noun)

   1. Twelve active and alert dogs drew *the sled*.[55]

   2. All *of those*, great and small, are *problems*, but can be resolved *with fortitude and a certain determination*.

   3. Another longer and *more* miserable silence was broken *by Cyril*.[56]

   4. *Many* colorful and bright balloons filled *the sky after the celebration*.

5. Possessive pronouns as adjectives

   1. Your *excessively* rude cousin pinched *me particularly hard*.

   2. Our post office closed.

   3. My adorable new kitten mewed *questioningly*.

   4. My dishwasher broke.

6. Indefinite pronouns acting as adjectives

   1. Many brides *before Queen Victoria* wore *black wedding dresses*.

   2. Another tribe *to the east* is *nomadic*.[57]

   3. Some giants may be *friendly*.

   4. Some people *in the celebrations* dye *their hair orange*.

7. Demonstrative pronouns as adjectives

   1. This take-it-or-leave-it avatar is *not typical of other styles of games*.[58]

   2. *Somewhere*, this *very* untidy room contains *my completely finished project*.

   3. Is this book *the right one*?

   4. These illnesses caused *many deaths* and caused *delays to the construction*.

---

55. *The Call of the Wild*, Jack London
56. *Five Children and It*, E. Nesbit
57. *The Histories* by Herodotus, translation by Aubrey de Sélincourt
58. *What is Your Quest?: From Adventure Games to Interactive Books*, Anastasia Salter

8. Interrogative pronouns as adjectives

    1. Which phone is ringing?

    2. Whose stomach is growling *so loudly?*

    3. Which house is *new*?

    4. What show is *your favorite?*

9. Past participles as adjectives

    1. Chipped teacups leak.

    2. A watched pot *never* boils.

    3. Our embarrassed neighbors bring *their dogs into the house.*

    4. The unearthed warriors were *facsimiles of the surrounding court.*

10. Present participles as adjectives

    1. Boiling water steeps *aromatic tea.*

    2. Flowering plants beautify *gardens.*

    3. My complaining father calls *our neighbors.*

    4. Hunting cheetahs prefer *night hours.*[59]

IIB. Adverbs

1. Adverbs that modify verbs

    1. Did they work diligently?

    2. The furious bull snorted menacingly.

    3. Today I breakfasted late.

    4. The movie ended abruptly.

---

59. *The Wild Cat Book*, Fiona and Mel Sunquist

2. Adverbs that modify adjectives

    1. Very talented Lily can jump *extremely* high.

    2. The extremely old chair wobbled threateningly.

    3. Earth's most powerful radio signal beams *from the Arecibo telescope.*

    4. Yesterday, some incredibly fragrant roses bloomed.

3. Adverbs that modify other adverbs

    1. Traffic stopped quite suddenly.

    2. She extended *her dress* still farther.[60]

    3. The freshman rather nervously addressed *the senior class.*

    4. Various cattle breeds differ very much.[61]

4. Compound adverbs (two or more adverbs modifying the same word)

    1. They crassly and dishonestly stole *Buck.*[62]

    2. A great fear seized *him* and contracted *his muscles* spasmodically and instinctively.[63]

    3. She ran busily to and fro.[64]

    4. The cat hunts quietly and cautiously.[65]

5. Interrogative adverbs (including pronouns)

    1. When did you eat *dinner?*

    2. Where are you going so hurriedly?

    3. Why should there be *a change?*[66]

    4. Where are we driving today?

---

60. *Rebecca of Sunnybrook Farm*, Kate Douglas Wiggin
61. *Home Life in All Lands,* Charles Morris
62. *The Call of the Wild*, Jack London
63. *The Call of the Wild*, Jack London
64. *Heidi*, Johanna Spyri
65. *Home Life in All Lands,* Charles Morris
66. *Heidi*, Johanna Spyri

6. Adverbs of affirmation

    1. She fell down and wept very loudly.[67]

    2. Yes, *dear reader,* you are *right.*[68]

    3. Yes, the Giant was *ready to do that,* and he turned *the six brothers into king's sons again, and their brides into king's daughters.*[69]

    4. The absolutely beautiful sunset was *orange and red.*

7. Adverbs of negation

    1. I will never forget *you.*

    2. I didn't make *a bad guess.*[70]

    3. The child does not look very *terrible.*[71]

    4. A cat's claws do not touch *the ground.*[72]

---

67. *Rebecca of Sunnybrook Farm*, Kate Douglas Wiggin

68. *The Sunny Side*, A. A. Milne

69. *A Book of Giants: Tales of Very Tall Men of Myth, Legend, History, and Science,* Henry Wysham Lanier

70. *Rebecca of Sunnybrook Farm*, Kate Douglas Wiggin

71. *Heidi,* Johanna Spyri

72. *Home Life in All Lands,* Charles Morris

PART III: HOW TO DIAGRAM PREPOSITIONAL PHRASES

IIIA. Prepositional phrases acting as modifiers

1. Prepositional phrases that act as adjectives

    1. Brides in India wear *red*.

    2. The people of Samos did not want *liberty*.[73]

    3. A turtle with a flaky shell may be *sick*.

    4. The number of deaths decreased rapidly.

2. Prepositional phrases that act as predicate adjectives

    > If you do not know how to diagram predicate adjectives, please see section V of *The Diagramming Dictionary*.

    1. The house on the secluded lane is on fire.

    2. Our flight is on time.

    3. A book about unicorns is on order.

    4. The hotel down the street is under construction.

3. Prepositional phrases modifying other prepositional phrases

    1. The seed is spread by birds on the tops of buildings.[74]

    2. The workers of the Central Pacific were now compensating for their years of slow, heavy labor in the mountains.[75]

    3. Among the trees in the deepest part of the forest lives the wise old owl.

    4. Many of the workers on the canal kept contracting *malaria and yellow fever.*

---

73. *The Histories*, Herodotus, translation by Aubrey de Sélincourt
74. *Punjab Plants*, J. L. Stewart
75. *The Transcontinental Railroad*, Thomas Streissguth

4. Prepositional phrases that act as adverbs

  1. Tom was panting with exertion by this time.[76]

  2. The European olive had been introduced into the Calcutta Botanical Gardens in 1800.[77]

  3. At one point, a suit was brought by the entire district against a tax-collector.[78]

  4. Perpetual nighttime thunderstorms occur in Lake Maracaibo.

IIIB. Prepositional phrases acting as nouns

1. Prepositional phrases that act as subjects

  1. In the south was *her lost home.*

  2. Beneath that tree is *my favorite spot.*

  3. Toward those trees is *your path.*

  4. In the wind is *bitterly cold.*

2. Prepositional phrases that act as direct objects

> If you do not know how to diagram direct objects, please see section IVA 1 of *The Diagramming Dictionary.*
>   If you do not know how to diagram objects, please see section IV of *The Diagramming Dictionary.*

  1. My grandmother told *me* about her childhood.

  2. I had never heard of that legend.

  3. The prisoner asked for mercy.

  4. Tell *him* about the mystery.

---

76. *The Adventures of Tom Sawyer*, Mark Twain
77. *Punjab Plants*
78. *Pompeii: The Living City*, Alex Butterworth and Ray Laurence

3. Prepositional phrases that act as predicate nominatives

> If you do not know how to diagram predicate nominatives yet, please see section VB of *The Diagramming Dictionary*.

1. My favorite ride is in a private jet.

2. The time for questions is before the exam.

3. My favorite spot is beneath that tree.

4. My favorite place is at the beach.

4. Prepositional phrases that act as objects of the preposition

1. A growl rumbled from beneath the roof.

2. Our father telephoned *us* from across the country.

3. Laura has been smiling since before the beginning of class.

4. The only way out of the labyrinth *of suffering* is to forgive.

IIIC. Objects of prepositions, special cases

1. Compound objects of prepositions

1. They talked lazily of this and that.

2. Unlike Augustus's organizations, Nero's new club did not revolve around piety, obedience, conformity, and respect.[79]

3. To his surprise and chagrin, everyone did not agree with him.[80]

4. We laughed about this and that.

2. Gerunds as objects of prepositions

1. I am very tired of travelling.

2. Tess earns extra money by coaching.

3. Why had he talked about churning butter?[81]

4. The greatest glory in living lies in rising.

---

79. *Pompeii: The Living City,* Alex Butterworth and Ray Laurence
80. *The Knights Hospitaller: A Military History of the Knights of St. John,* by John C. Carr
81. *Otto of the Silver Hand,* Howard Pyle

PART IV: OBJECTS

IVA. Direct Objects

1. Direct objects

    1. Aunt Lou fixes especially fine meals.

    2. Bonnie and Reginald settled their differences yesterday.

    3. You left your hat here yesterday.

    4. I quickly dropped the hot pan.

2. Compound direct objects

    1. Buck didn't read the newspapers or journals.[82]

    2. Do not forget this letter and that ring.

    3. You will see the mink and the fox in repose.[83]

    4. Then old Mrs. Rabbit took a basket and her umbrella.[84]

3. Compound predicates with compound direct objects

    1. Tom eagerly drew his sore toe from the sheet and held it up for inspection.[85]

    2. Our neighbors were playing baseball earlier and accidentally broke Mr. Larson's window.

    3. He prided himself on his simple manner of living and never exacted any pay.[86]

    4. It would shorten a ship's journey and avoid travel around Cape Horn.

---

82. *The Call of the Wild,* Jack London
83. *What the Robin Knows,* Jon Young
84. *The Tale of Peter Rabbit,* Beatrix Potter
85. *The Adventures of Tom Sawyer,* Mark Twain
86. *The Library of the World's Best Literature, Ancient and Modern,* Vol. 12, ed. Charles Dudley Warner

4. Compound predicates with the same direct object

    1. The sights tantalized and tempted me to outspoken treason.

    2. Stamp and deliver this important letter!

    3. The Working Men they spared but decimated.[87]

    4. Before the party, we baked and decorated the chocolate cupcakes.

5. Interrogative pronouns as direct objects

    1. Whom have you asked?

    2. She ate what?

    3. She bought what?

    4. Whom did the dog bite?

6. Demonstrative pronouns as direct objects

    1. Who made this?

    2. I am pointing this out.

    3. Who wore this?

    4. She said that.

7. Gerunds as direct objects

    1. I love eating.[88]

    2. I don't mind lying, but I hate inaccuracy.[89]

> If you do not know how to diagram independent clauses, please see section VIB 1 of *The Diagramming Dictionary.*

    3. Stop shouting.

    4. Shang Yang began conquering.

---

87. *FLATLAND: A Romance of Many Dimensions*, Edwin A. Abbott
88. Wang Meng
89. Samuel Butler

8. Infinitives as direct objects

    1. The old soldier did not fear to die.[90]

    2. We must learn to live or to perish.[91]

    3. I cannot bear to witness any longer.

    4. Teach yourself to be.

9. Compound nouns or proper names as direct objects

    1. Aunt Debbie taught me Polish.

    2. Anne met her Waterloo.[92]

    3. Zoe regarded the overly eager salesman suspiciously.

    4. The goose's loud noises can arouse the entire household.[93]

10. Understood relative pronoun acting as a direct object

> If you are unaware of how to diagram a dependent clause, please see section VIC of *The Diagramming Dictionary*.

> *The Diagramming Dictionary* recommends placing an *x* in the place of the understood relative pronoun when diagramming, but you can also add the understood relative pronoun in parentheses. Both methods are provided in the answer key, one method per sentence.

    1. The feast *that evening* was surely the merriest the castle had ever seen.[94]

    2. Beside the volcano Annika made is my project.

    3. The giraffe we saw was *extremely tall and ravenously hungry.*

    4. In the cookies Jamal made are nuts and chocolate chunks.

---

90. Alexandre Dumas
91. Martin Luther King Jr.
92. *Anne of Green Gables*, L. M. Montgomery
93. *Home Life in All Lands*, Charles Morris
94. *The Castle of Llyr*, Lloyd Alexander

11. Appositive nouns after direct objects

> 1. Her stockings, her stockings I have sold for drink.[95]
>
> 2. *I believe Hoggs*–I mean my cousin Howard–*was coming down specially to meet him.*[96]
>
> 3. *Tell Mildred* I got a beautiful Dutch doll for little Emma Jones–one of those *crying* babies *that can open and shut their eyes and turn their head.*[97]
>
> 4. In 1866, Fry launched a dark chocolate bar *filled with a mint fondant:* Fry's Chocolate Cream.[98]

12. Object complements (both object complement nouns and object complement adjectives)

Nouns:

> 1. The teacher appointed you monitor.
>
> 2. The instructor declared Marisa his apprentice.
>
> 3. Arnold pronounced the event a success.
>
> 4. They called the painting a masterpiece.

Adjectives:

> 1. She found the situation perplexing.
>
> 2. The circus made the children happy.
>
> 3. We found the old house empty.
>
> 4. We painted the walls blue.

95. *Crime and Punishment*, Fyodor Dostoyevsky
96. *The Man Who Knew Too Much*, G. K. Chesterton
97. From a letter from Robert E. Lee to his wife, Mary (1856)
98. *Sweets: A History of Candy*, Tim Richardson

IVB. Indirect objects

1. Indirect objects

    1. Sean bought us brunch.

    2. The artist sold him a unique painting.

    3. I made you a quilt.

    4. Arianna drew me a lovely picture.

2. Compound indirect objects

    If you haven't learned how to diagram proper nouns, see the next set of examples (section IVB. 3 in *The Diagramming Dictionary*).

    1. She gave me and my brother hugs and kisses.

    2. Gwendolen showed Rachna and Ethan the secret passage.

    3. Sierra gave her friends and family homemade treats.

    4. I asked Sara and Dylan the questions.

3. Proper nouns as indirect objects

    1. Uncle Walter mailed Joey the cookies.

    2. The instructor gave Marisa an apprenticeship.

    3. Jordan gave Sophia a treat.

    4. The king offered Anne Boleyn a crown.

PART V: PREDICATE ADJECTIVES AND PREDICATE NOMINATIVES

VA. Predicate adjectives

1. Predicate adjective

   1. Are you afraid?

   2. Kittens are adorable.

   3. The dark cellar was not inviting.

   4. The cave exploration was exciting!

2. Compound predicate adjectives

   1. Barter can be complex and problematic.

   2. He seemed most assured and trustful.[99]

   3. Tomorrow, we shall be richer and more powerful.[100]

   4. Tonight's sunset is bright orange and red.

3. Prepositional phrases as predicate adjectives

   1. The best time for us is after dinner.

   2. All of this is on account of us.[101]

   3. Alan is in love with Rita.

   4. You are in a bad mood.

---

99. *Henry VIII*, J.J. Scarisbrick
100. "The Devil to Pay," Dorothy Sayers
101. *The Civil Rights Movement,* Elizabeth Sirimarco

VB. Predicate nominatives

1. Predicate nominatives

    1. Most bats are insectivores.

    2. Be a good sport!

    3. A golden ticket was an exciting prospect.

    4. Her studio was an old barn.

2. Compound predicate nominatives

    1. Nantucket was her great original, the Tyre of this Carthage, the place *where the first dead American whale was stranded.*[102]

    2. Dr. Quinn was a plain, honest creature and a man *to whom I would have gone.*[103]

    3. At the same time, they were your adversary, your nemesis, your mortal enemy.[104]

    4. The villain in the story is probably neither Cambyses nor Darius.[105]

3. Infinitives as predicate nominatives

    1. To give is to receive.[106]

    2. The plan for the day is to relax.

    3. The goal of this class is to learn.

    4. The secret of success is to do.

---

102. *Moby Dick*, Herman Melville
103. *A Thin Ghost and Others*, M. R. James
104. *Barbarian Days: A Surfing Life*, William Finnegan
105. *The History of the Ancient World*, Susan Wise Bauer
106. Raymond Holliwell

PART VI: PHRASES AND CLAUSES

VIA. Phrases

1. Verb phrases

    1. The new tadpoles were wriggling furiously.

    2. Will you read me a story?

    3. Has she answered knowledgeably?

    4. Tonight, the play will end dramatically.

2. Gerunds and infinitive phrases as direct objects

    1. The King of Persia planned to destroy both him and his tribe.

    2. They preferred to build their own house.[107]

    3. No knight in those days dared to ride the roads without full armor.[108]

    4. The entire gymnastics team enjoyed competing as a group and as individuals.

3. Gerund and infinitive phrases as subjects

    1. To ignore the Romans is not just to turn a blind eye to the distant past.[109]

    2. Playing the difficult piece was quite an accomplishment for the young violinist.

    3. Running a marathon was one of Jamison's goals.

    4. To end the dispute was old Dame Scarecrow's aim.[110]

---

107. *The Matchlock Gun*, Walter D. Edmonds
108. *Otto of the Silver Hand*, Howard Pyle
109. *SPQR: A History of Ancient Rome*, Mary Beard
110. *A Wonder Book for Girls and Boys*, Nathaniel Hawthorne

4. Gerund and infinitive phrases as predicate nominatives

1. *Space can bend and twist and stretch, and* probably the best way *to think about space* is to imagine a big piece of rubber *that you can twist.*[111]

2. The scientist's achievement was discovering a new comet.

3. The jobs of the lab assistant were keeping track of the supplies needed and restocking them.

4. An apparently more modest path was to use the method of the "table-makers," *as they were called, not as a condensed and convenient way to present chemical knowledge, but as an end in itself.*[112]

5. Participle and infinitive phrases as predicate adjectives

1. The dark cave appeared to be full of snakes and spiders.

2. Now he seemed absorbed in examining his powder horn and filling it from the big horn beside the chimney.[113]

3. He was to leave the happy, sunny silence of the dear White Cross and to go out into that great world.[114]

4. The stick seemed to be alive in his hand, and to lend some of its life to Perseus.[115]

---

111. Alan Guth

112. *A History of Chemistry*, Bernadette Bensaude-Vincent and Isabelle Stengers, translated by Deborah van Dam

113. *The Matchlock Gun*, Walter D. Edmonds

114. *Otto of the Silver Hand*, Howard Pyle

115. *A Wonder Book for Girls and Boys*, Nathaniel Hawthorne

VIB. Independent Clauses

1. Multiple Independent Clauses

   1. From the depths of the packing case, he suddenly heard a faint "Ork," and his heart stood still.[116]

   2. Government is the badge of lost innocence; the palaces of kings are built on the ruins of the bowers of paradise.[117]

   3. The wind was now behind them, so they didn't have to shout.[118]

   4. There was no pot of yellow rice and fish, and the boy knew this, too.[119]

VIC. Dependent Clauses

1. Dependent clauses acting as adjectives

   ### Relative adjective clauses

   1. I am meeting Shirin, whose textbook I borrowed.

   2. The birthday cake that Sarah made for Fritz was absolutely delicious!

   3. He held several long conversations with old women whom we met.[120]

   4. The admiral was one for whom decisiveness had always been a career hallmark.[121]

---

116. *Mr. Popper's Penguins*, Richard and Florence Atwater

117. *Common Sense*, Thomas Paine

118. *The House at Pooh Corner*, A.A. Milne

119. *The Old Man and the Sea*, Ernest Hemingway

120. *A Thin Ghost and Others*, M. R. James

121. *The Essential Novels: Star Wars Legends 10-Book Bundle*, published by Random House in 2012

Relative adverb clauses

1. He scarce heeds the moment when he drops seething into the yawning jaws awaiting him.[122]

2. The book was written at a time when faraway lands were mysterious to many Europeans.

3. He was afflicted by a continual discontent with the height of the table where he worked.[123]

4. There were times when it had been so cold.[124]

2. Dependent clauses acting as adverbs

1. Although the courier made a great noise, Baisemeaux heard nothing.[125]

2. Since no practical good could result from it, I did not tell all that I knew.[126]

3. When nonviolence becomes a reality, it is a powerful force.[127]

4. We were able to make better time because we had his trail to follow.[128]

122. *Moby Dick*, Herman Melville
123. *Bartleby, The Scrivener*, Herman Melville
124. *The Namesake*, Jhumpa Lahiri
125. *The Man in the Iron Mask*, Alexandre Dumas
126. *The Hound of the Baskervilles*, Arthur Conan Doyle
127. *Nonviolence: The History of a Dangerous Idea*, Mark Kurlansky
128. *A Negro Explorer at the North Pole*, Memoir written by Matthew Henson

3. Dependent clauses acting as nouns

Noun clause as subject

1. How students could apply for college was the topic of our meeting.

2. What you want to do is to write a really long letter to Mrs. Cardew, acquainting her with all the facts.[129]

3. Where Tarzan stood was dark.[130]

4. Whatever secret hope had agitated him was quickly dispelled by Dorothy's next speech.[131]

Noun clause as direct object

1. None of them could understand how a child could be so slow and backward in learning to care for itself.[132]

2. I scooped up some of the sand and saw that it was really tiny sapphires that made noises like laughter when I rubbed some of them between my palms.[133]

3. You cannot do a kindness too soon, for you never know how soon it will be too late.[134]

4. Each thought there was one cat too many.[135]

Noun clause as predicate nominative

1. The most extraordinary development was when the reindeer and the wolf snuggled together.

2. In 1918, if you heard a neighbor or a relation coughing or saw them fall down in front of you, you knew there was a good chance that you were already sick yourself.[136]

3. Compassion and strength are what we are, and we have translated these into every area of our existence because we have had to.[137]

---

129. *The Sunny Side*, A. A. Milne
130. *The Return of Tarzan*, Edgar Rice Burroughs
131. *Twice-Told Tales,* Nathaniel Hawthorne
132. *Tarzan of the Apes*, Edgar Rice Burroughs
133. *Dragonwings*, Laurence Yep
134. Ralph Waldo Emerson
135. A traditional Irish song
136. *Pale Rider: The Spanish Flu of 1918 and How it Changed the World*, Laura Spinney
137. Jeannette Armstrong

4. The secret of this phenomenon was that hatred had become the enjoyment of the wretch's soul.[138]

Noun clause as object of the preposition

1. A good farmer must be quick in his judgment of what should be done at the present time, and he should have a good perception to show him the best thing to do for the future.[139]

2. I have previously written about how much we are affected by atmospheres here, and I think that in my own case this trouble is getting much worse lately.[140]

3. Less than a year elapsed before Attica was invaded, and the war openly began.[141]

4. His disregard for what he was saying, when he was saying it, and to whom he was saying it was alarming.[142]

Noun clause as appositive

1. It is a good thing that scorpions are so destructive to each other, or they would multiply so greatly as to make some countries uninhabitable.[143]

2. It is calculated that eleven hundred persons have at different times suffered death rather than break their eggs at the smaller end.[144]

3. Little Jackal wanted to attend, but there was a law made that no one should be present unless he had horns.[145]

4. The rumor, that Belle had been the child of an illegitimate relationship, would persist in the Frost family.[146]

138. *Twice-Told Tales,* Nathaniel Hawthorne
139. *Prairie Farmer: A Weekly Journal for the Farm, Orchard and Fireside*
140. *The Diary of a Young Girl,* Anne Frank, translated by B. M. Mooyaart
141. *The History of the Peloponnesian War,* Thucydides
142. *The Strivers' Row Spy,* Jason Overstreet
143. *A History of the Earth and Animated Nature,* Oliver Goldsmith
144. *Gulliver's Travels,* Jonathan Swift
145. *South African Folk Tales,* James A. Honey
146. *Robert Frost: A Life,* Jay Parini

PART VII: FILLING UP THE CORNERS

1. Parenthetical elements

    1. Quietness and value–Jim and the chain had quietness and value.[147]

    2. Aunt Hester went out once–where or for what I do not know–and happened to be absent when my master desired her presence.[148]

    3. She laughed softly with a strange quality in the sound–it was a laugh of happiness–and of content–and of misery.[149]

    4. Death and mortal illness, in Rome, was not especially associated with old age (and very few of Galen's recorded patients are old), nor even necessarily with childhood.[150]

2. Noun of direct address

    1. *Oh,* Squire, we should have followed you through fire and flood, to be sure.[151]

    2. Mowgli, hast thou anything to say?[152]

    3. *Oh,* Ashley, I love you so much that I'd walk every step of the way to Virginia just to be near you![153]

    4. *No,* Dana, I just didn't pay any attention.[154]

---

147. "The Gift of the Magi," O. Henry

148. *Narrative of the Life of Frederick Douglass*, Frederick Douglass

149. "A Ramble in Aphasia," O. Henry

150. *The Prince of Medicine: Galen in the Roman Empire*, Susan Mattern

151. *Waverley*, Sir Walter Scott

152. *The Jungle Book*, Rudyard Kipling

153. *Gone with the Wind*, Margaret Mitchell

154. *Kindred*, Octavia Butler

3. Interjection

    1. Alas, Mr. Waverley, I have no better advice.[155]

    2. Well, if I am a man, a man I must become.[156]

    3. Why, honey, of course there's going to be a war.[157]

    4. Hm, tide's running strong tonight.[158]

4. Phrases as appositives

    1. To look up the antecedents of all these people, to discover their
       bona fides–that takes time and endless inconvenience.[159]

    2. I think it would be a good plan to elect Raggedy Ann as our leader
       on this expedition.[160]

    3. Gran tells her about the various people who are en route right
       now, aunts, uncles.[161]

    4. If one of the players gets greedy and plays one defection too many,
       the other player will employ a so-called trigger strategy: to defect
       forever after.[162]

5. Absolute constructions

    1. Round her neck was a collar of very large pearls which,
       improbable though it seemed, were real.[163]

    2. Morton had just placed himself in front of the nearest window,
       his broad shoulders blocking the aperture.[164]

    3. That feels much better–a marvelous sense of security.[165]

    4. This pencil–a natty scarlet, as you observe, with gold lettering–
       didn't come from any of Darling's branches.[166]

---

155. *Waverley*, Sir Walter Scott
156. *The Jungle Book,* Rudyard Kipling
157. *Gone with the Wind*, Margaret Mitchell
158. *The Jungle Book*, Rudyard Kipling
159. *Murder on the Orient Express*, Agatha Christie
160. *Raggedy Ann Stories*, Johnny Gruelle
161. *If I Stay*, Gayle Forman
162. *The Complete Idiot's Guide to Game Theory*, Edward Rosenthal
163. *Murder on the Orient Express*, Agatha Christie
164. *The Man Who Knew Too Much*, G. K. Chesterton
165. *Gaudy Night*, Dorothy Sayers
166. *Murder Must Advertise*, Dorothy Sayers

KEY

PART I: HOW TO DIAGRAM THE SIMPLE SUBJECT AND SIMPLE PREDICATE OF A SENTENCE

IA. Simple subjects

1. Common nouns as subjects

   1.   Meteorologists | issue

   2.   elephant | entered

   3.   hedgehog | hijacked

   4.   rain | fell

2. The understood you as subject

   1.   (you) | Learn

   2.   (you) | Eat

3. (you) | Mail

4. (you) | Close

3. Pronouns as subjects

1. you | Are

2. I | see

3. He | stood

4. I | mowed

4. Compound nouns as subjects

1. trout fishing | succeeds
         \Early

2.

3.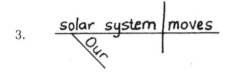

4.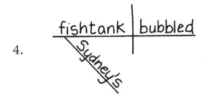

5. Compound subjects

1.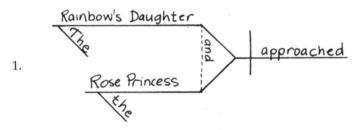

2.

Alexandra
Raphael and | play

3.

Water
nutrients and | are

4.

6. Compound subjects with more than one coordinating conjunction

1.
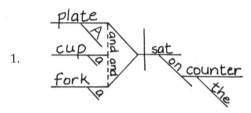

2.
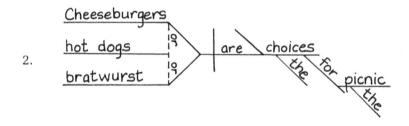

3.
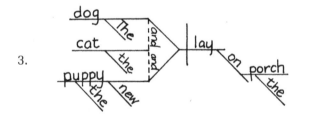

4.
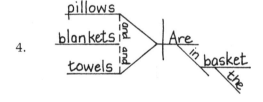

7. Proper nouns as subjects

1.   Juliana | recycles

2.   Marie Curie | researched

3.   Louisa May Alcott | wrote

4.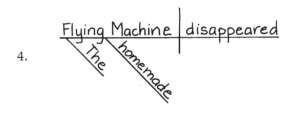

8. Indefinite pronouns as subjects

1.   Nobody | knows | him

2.   Something | did happen

3.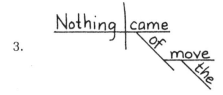

4.   Few | are \ angels

9. Prepositional phrases as subjects

1.

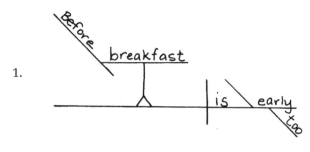

2.

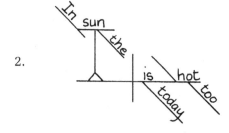

3.

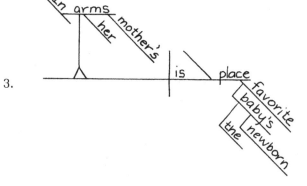

4.

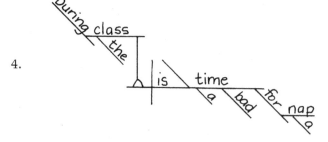

10. Demonstrative pronouns as subjects

1.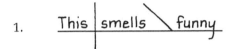

2.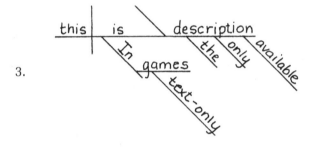

3.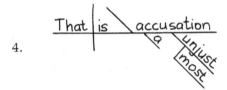

4.

11. Interrogative pronouns as subjects

1.

2.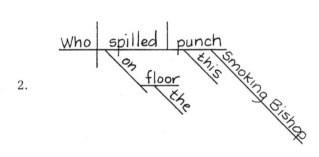

3.

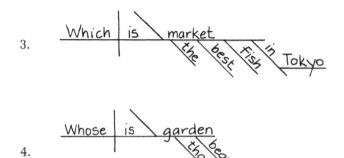

4.

12. Contractions as subjects

1.

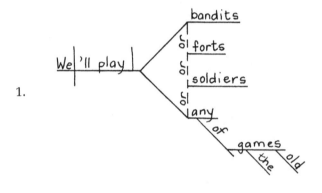

2.

3.

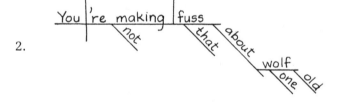

4.

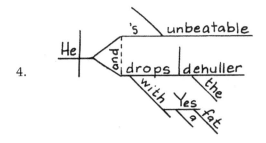

13. Intensive pronouns with a subject

1.

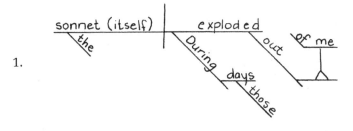

2.

3.

4.

14. Gerunds as subjects

1.

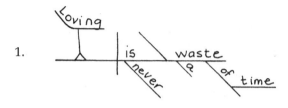

2.

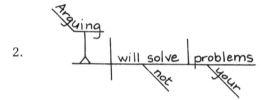

3.

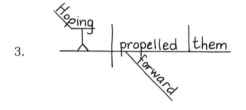

4.

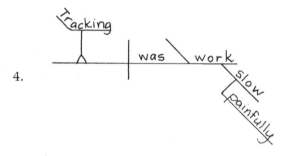

15. Infinitives as subjects

1.

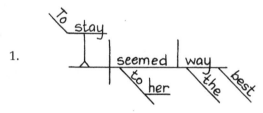

2.

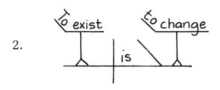

3.

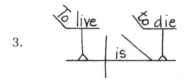

4.

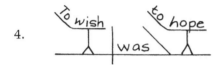

16. Compound subjects with coordinating correlative conjunctions

1.

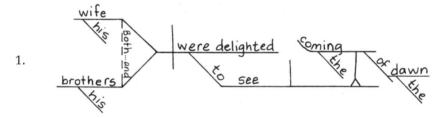

2.

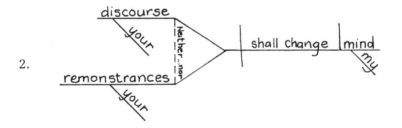

3.

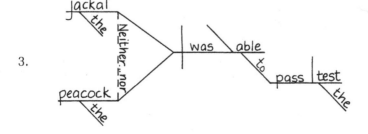

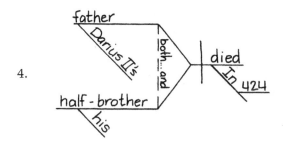

4.

17. Appositive nouns after subjects

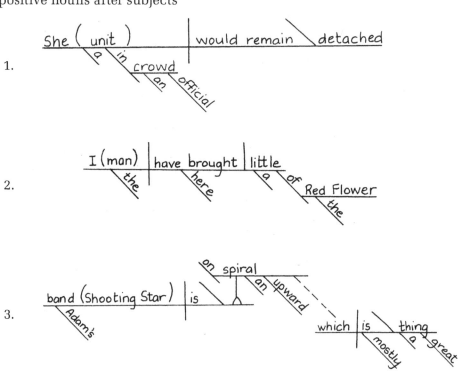

1.

2.

3.

NOTE: In case you are wondering about how the predicate of this sentence is diagrammed, here's our explanation.

Although you may want to diagram *on an upward spiral* as an adverb phrase, since *is* is a linking verb, it makes more sense to diagram the prepositional phrase as a predicate adjective.

4.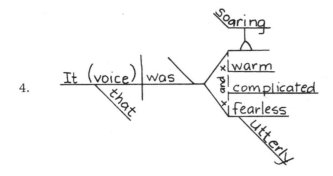

18. Unknown subjects with hortative verbs

1.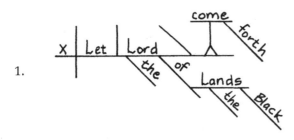

2.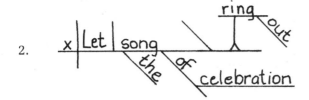

3.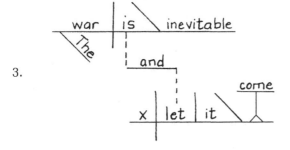

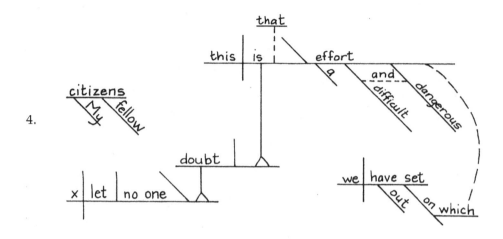

4.

1B. Simple predicates

1. Helping verbs

1.   He | was swimming

2.   Oliver | was talking

3.   She | was thinking

4.   Squirrels | will gather

2. Compound predicates

1.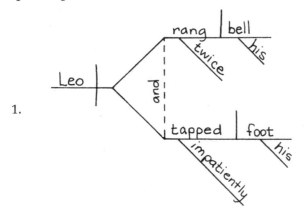

2.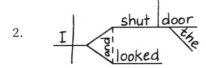

3.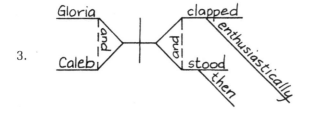

4.

3. Compound predicates with more than one coordinating conjunction

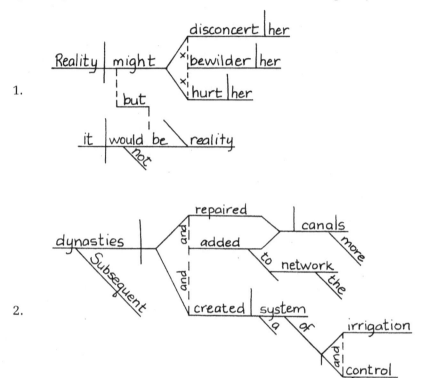

NOTE: It is acceptable to diagram *flood control* as a single compound noun.

3.

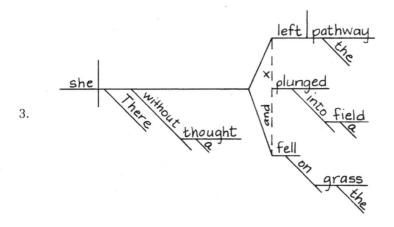

NOTE: You may choose to place an *X* to represent the comma on the dotted line between *left* and *plunged*. Additionally, if you're wondering about the phrase *There, without a thought*, we've diagrammed it as though it modifies all three verbs. An adverb modifying more than one verb can be placed after the verb-dividing line on the diagram, but before the branches of the compound verbs. A person could also simply diagram the phrase under *left*.

4.

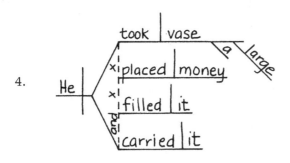

4. Contractions as predicates

1.

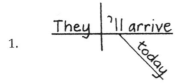

2.

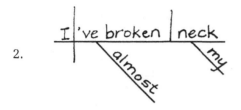

3.

4.

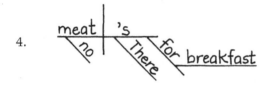

5. The understood helping verb

1.

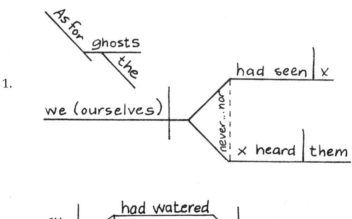

2.

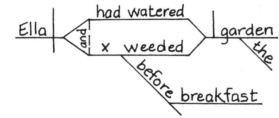

3.

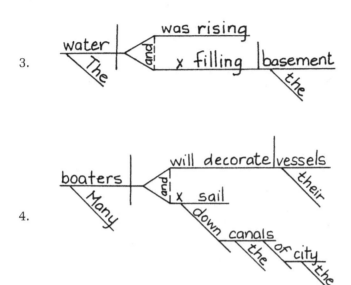

4.

6. Quasi-coordinators joining compound predicates

1.

2.

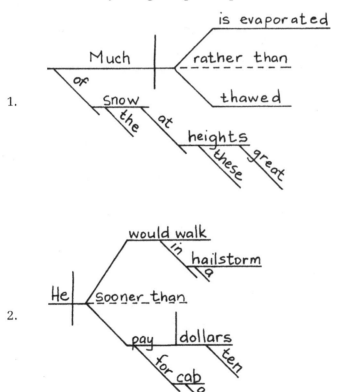

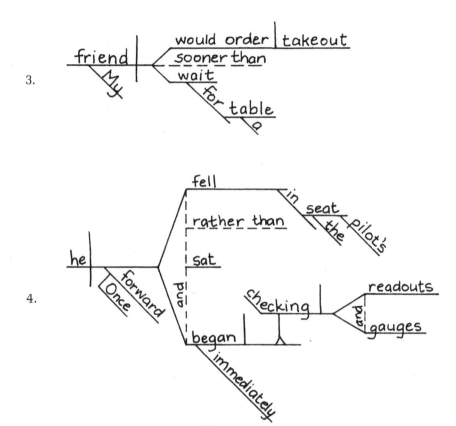

3.

4.

NOTE: The subject *he* is followed by three predicates: *fell, sat, and began*.
The first two are linked with the quasi-coordinator, the third by *and*.
The adverb *forward* (modified by *once*) modifies all three predicates (all
three actions happened once he was forward).

PART II: HOW TO DIAGRAM ADJECTIVES AND ADVERBS

IIA. Adjectives

1. Descriptive Adjectives

1.
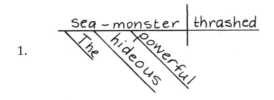

2.
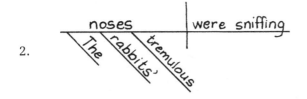

3.
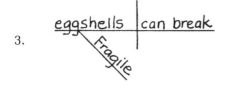

4.

music box | played

2. Compound adjectives (single adjectives made up of more than one word)

1.

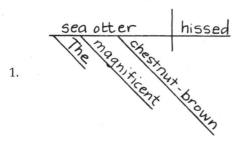

2.

3.

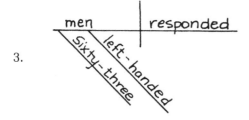

4.

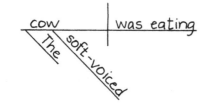

3. Articles

1.

2.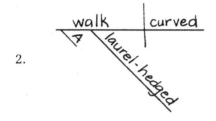

3.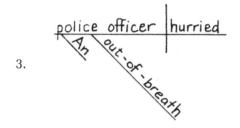

4.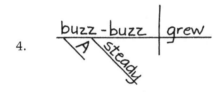

4. Compound adjectives (two or more adjectives modifying the same noun)

1.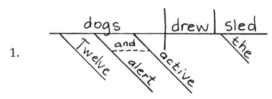

2.

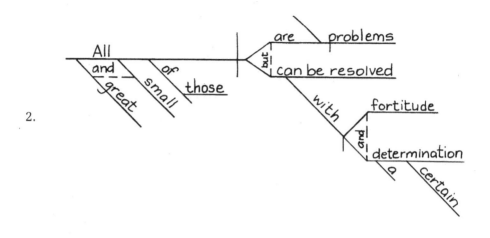

3.

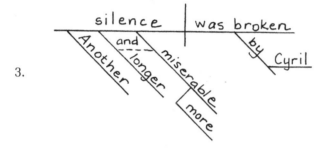

4.

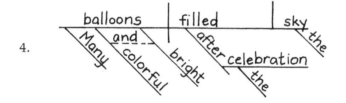

5. Possessive pronouns as adjectives

1.

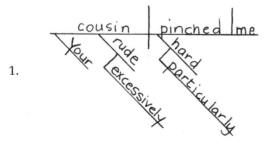

2.

3.

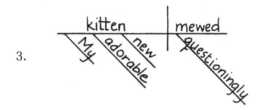

4.

6. Indefinite pronouns acting as adjectives

1.

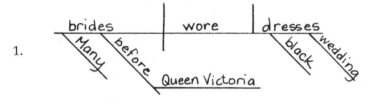

2.

3.

4.
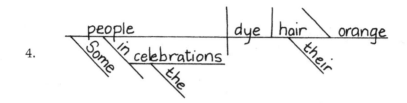

7. Demonstrative pronouns as adjectives

1.
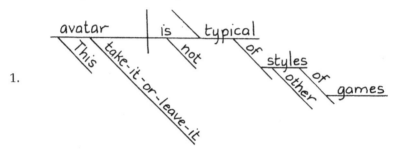

2.

3.

4.

8. Interrogative pronouns as adjectives

1.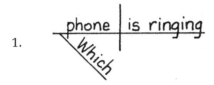

2.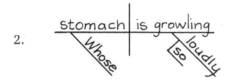

3.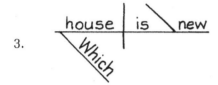

4.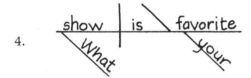

9. Past participles as adjectives

1.

2.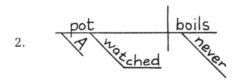

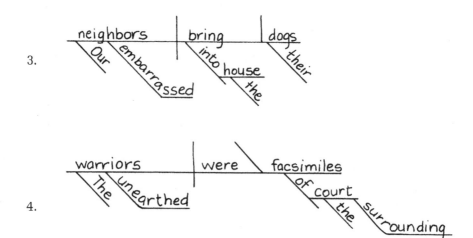

3.

4.

10. Present participles as adjectives

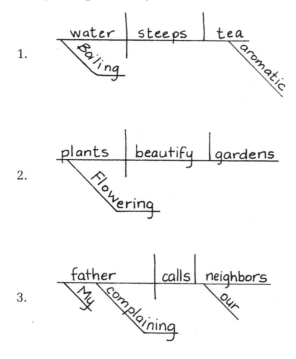

1.

2.

3.

4.

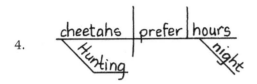

IIB. Adverbs

1. Adverbs that modify verbs

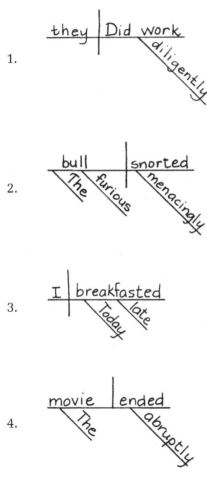

1.

2.

3.

4.

2. Adverbs that modify adjectives

1.

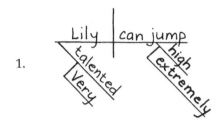

2.

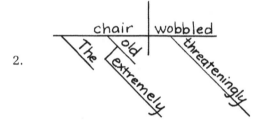

3.

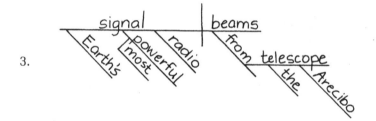

4.

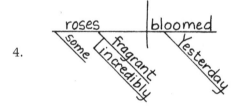

3. Adverbs that modify other adverbs

1.

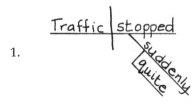

2.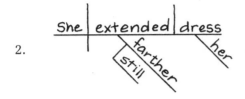

3.

4.

4. Compound adverbs (two or more adverbs modifying the same word)

1.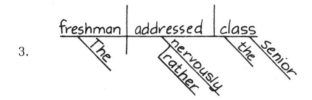

2.

3.
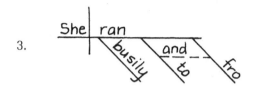

4.
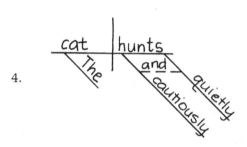

5. Interrogative adverbs (including pronouns)

1.
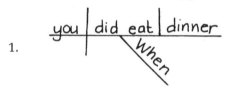

2.
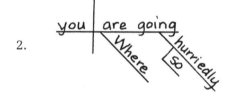

3.

4.

we | are driving
Where today

6. Adverbs of affirmation

1.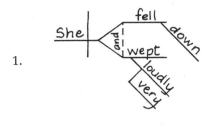

2.

reader
dear

you | are \ right
Yes

3.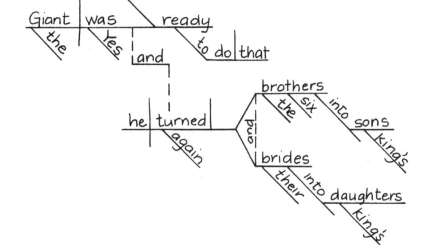

4.

sunset | was
The beautiful absolutely
and
orange
red

7. Adverbs of negation

1.

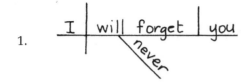

2.

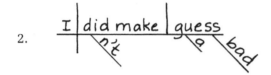

3.

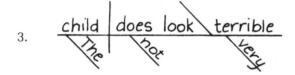

4.

PART III: HOW TO DIAGRAM PREPOSITIONAL PHRASES

IIIA. Prepositional phrases acting as modifiers

1. Prepositional phrases that act as adjectives

1.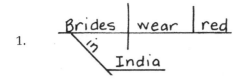

2.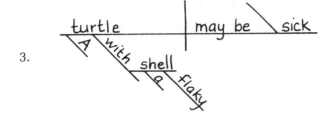

3.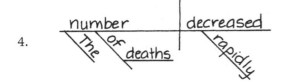

4.

2. Prepositional phrases that act as predicate adjectives

1.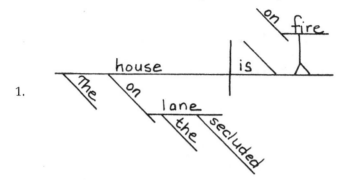

2.

3.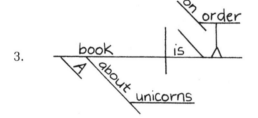

4.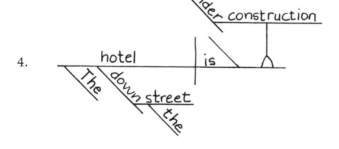

3. Prepositional phrases modifying other prepositional phrases

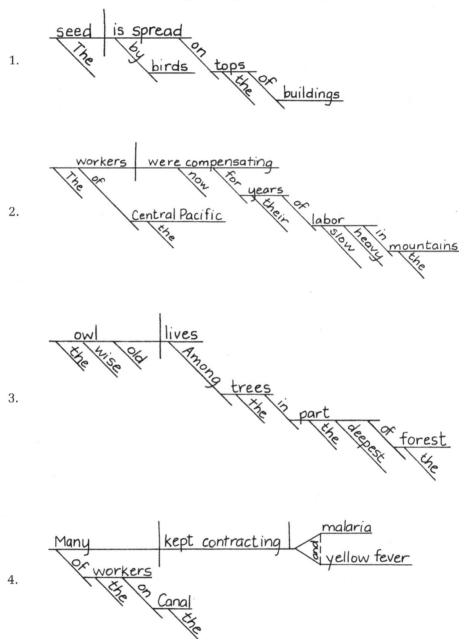

4. Prepositional phrases that act as adverbs

1.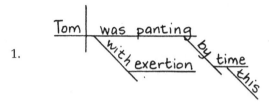

2.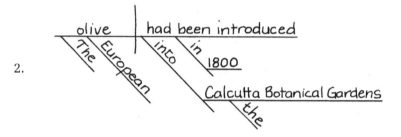

3.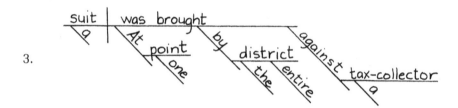

4.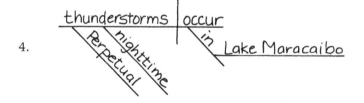

IIIB. Prepositional phrases acting as nouns

1. Prepositional phrases that act as subjects

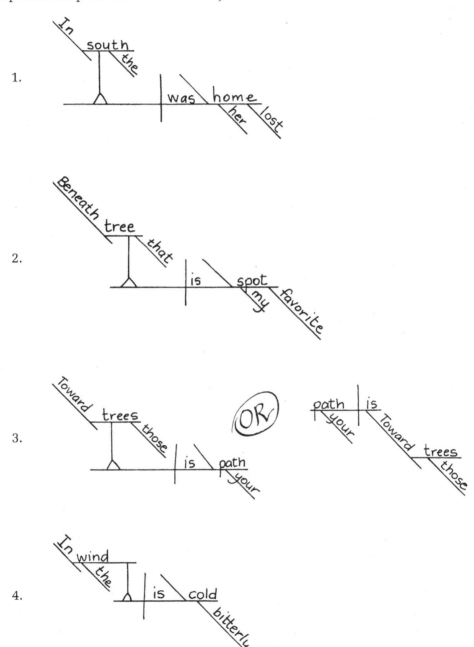

2. Prepositional phrases that act as direct objects

1.

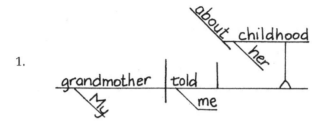

2.

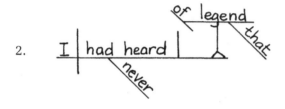

3.

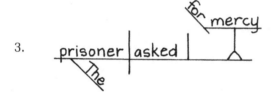

4.

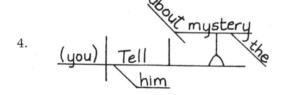

3. Prepositional phrases that act as predicate nominatives

1.

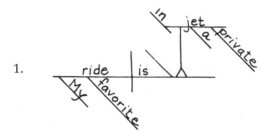

2.

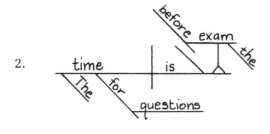

3.

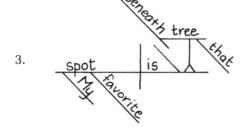

4.

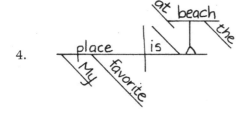

4. Prepositional phrases that act as objects of the preposition

1.

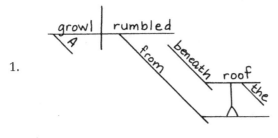

2.

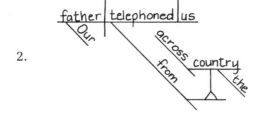

3.

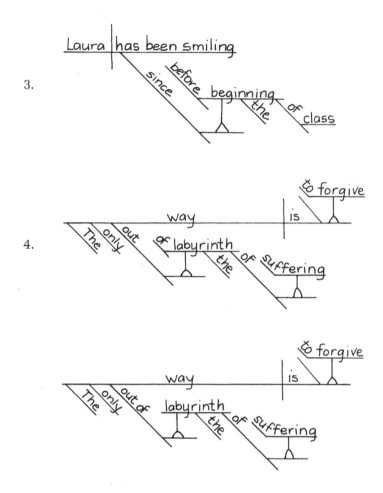

IIIC. Objects of prepositions, special cases

1. Compound objects of prepositions

1.

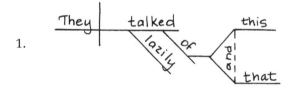

2.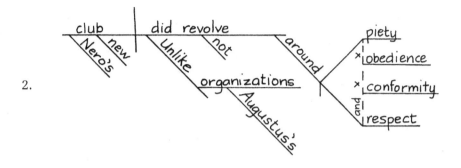

3.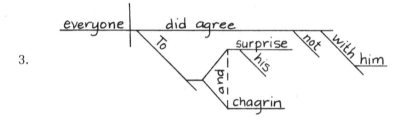

4.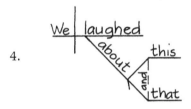

2. Gerunds as objects of prepositions

1.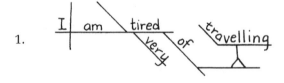

2.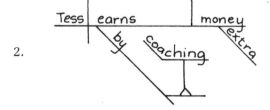

3.

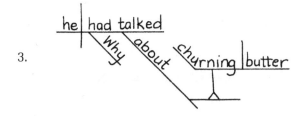

4.

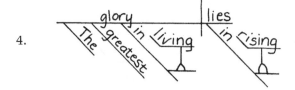

PART IV: OBJECTS

IVA. Direct Objects

1. Direct objects

1.

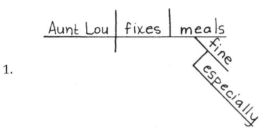

2.

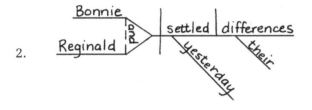

3.

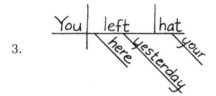

4.

2. Compound direct objects

1.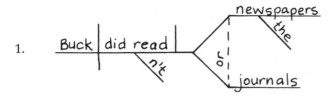

2.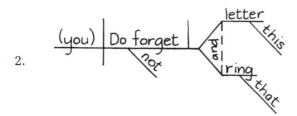

3.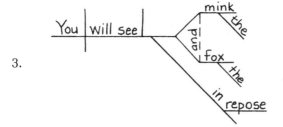

4.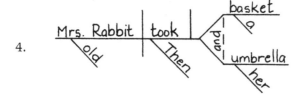

3. Compound predicates with compound direct objects

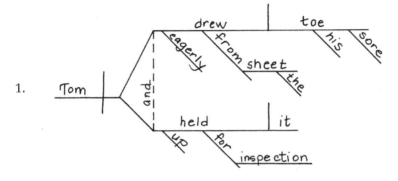

1.

2.

3.

4.

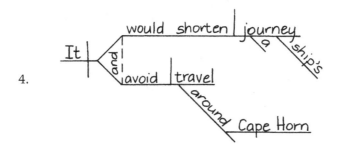

4. Compound predicates with the same direct object

1.

2.

3.

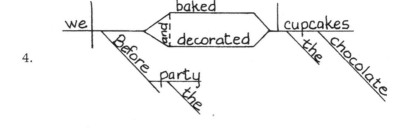

4.

5. Interrogative pronouns as direct objects

1. you | have asked | Whom

2. She | ate | what

3. She | bought | what

4. dog _{the} | did bite | Whom

6. Demonstrative pronouns as direct objects

1. Who | made | this

2. I | am pointing \ out | this

3. Who | wore | this

4. She | said | that

7. Gerunds as direct objects

1.
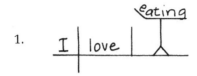

2.
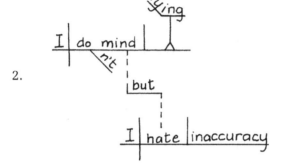

3.
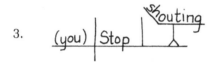

4.

8. Infinitives as direct objects

1.
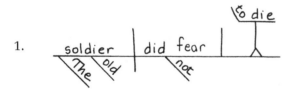

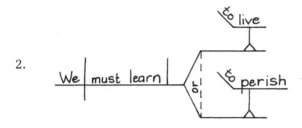

2.

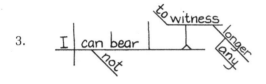

3.

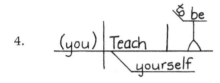

4.

9. Compound nouns or proper names as direct objects

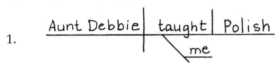

1.

2.

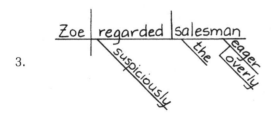

3.

4.

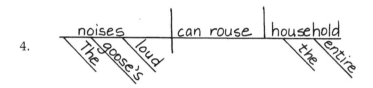

10. Understood relative pronoun acting as direct object

1.

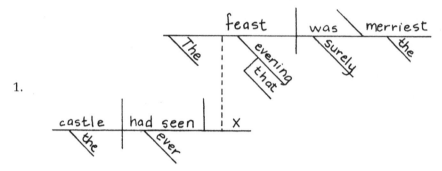

NOTE: The phrase *that evening* can be diagrammed as an adjective phrase modifying *feast*, or as a participle phrase with an understood *[held] that evening* (or perhaps *[happening] that evening*), in which case it becomes an adverb phrase answering the question *when*. *Evening* can be an adjective, but not, on its own, an adverb.

2.

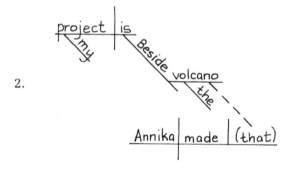

3.

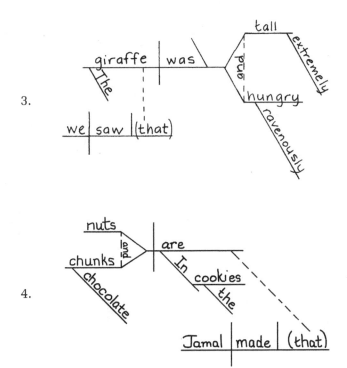

4.

11. Appositive nouns after direct objects

1.

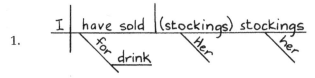

2.

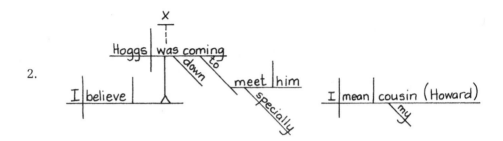

Note: *Specially* could also be diagrammed beneath *was coming*, since it is ambiguous whether he was *coming down specially*, or whether he was coming down *specially to meet him*.

3.

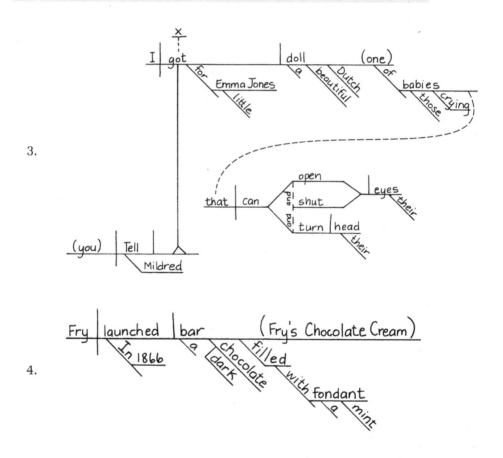

4.

12. Object complements (both object complement nouns and object
complement adjectives)

Nouns:

1. The teacher | appointed | you \ monitor

2. The instructor | declared | Marisa \ apprentice his

3. Arnold | pronounced | event the \ success a

4. They | called | painting the \ masterpiece a

Adjectives:

1. She | found | situation the \ perplexing

2. The circus | made | children the \ happy

3. We | found | house the old \ empty

4.

IVB. Indirect objects

1. Indirect objects

> NOTE: Indirect objects can be diagrammed with or without a tail
> (both options are seen in traditional diagramming guides and we show
> both options throughout our diagrams). Choose the style that works
> best for you.

1.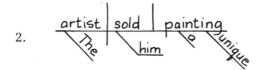

2. Compound indirect objects

1.
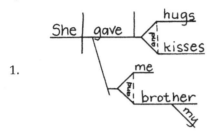

2.
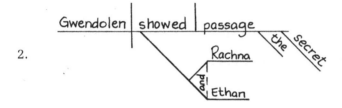

3.
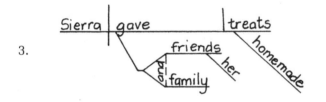

4.
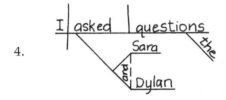

3. Proper nouns as indirect objects

1.

2.
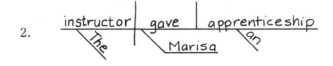

3.
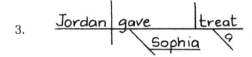

4.

king | offered | crown
The
Anne Boleyn

PART V: PREDICATE ADJECTIVES AND PREDICATE NOMINATIVES

VA. Predicate adjectives

1. Predicate adjective

1.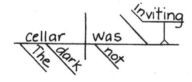

you | Are \ afraid

2. Kittens | are \ adorable

3. cellar | was \ inviting
   The dark not

   cellar | was inviting
   The dark not

> NOTE: *inviting* can be diagrammed as a predicate adjective or as a participle. Both options are demonstrated here.

4.

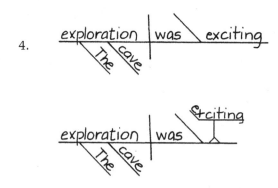

NOTE: *exciting* can be diagrammed as a predicate adjective or as a participle. Both options are demonstrated here.

2. Compound predicate adjectives

1.

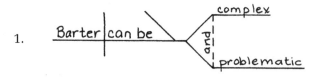

2.

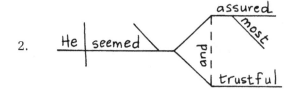

NOTE: "seemed" is acting as a linking verb.

3.

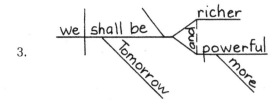

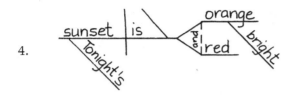

4.

3. Prepositional phrases as predicate adjectives

1.

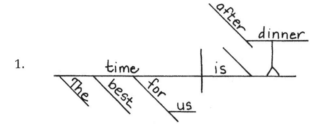

2.

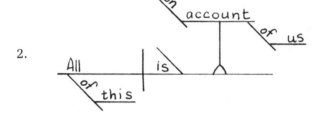

3.

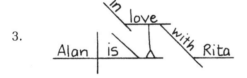

4.

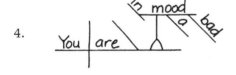

VB. Predicate nominatives

1. Predicate nominatives

1.

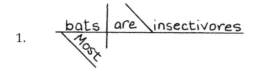

2.

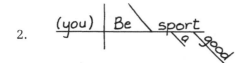

3.

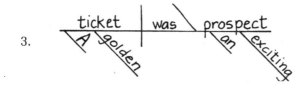

4.

2. Compound predicate nominatives

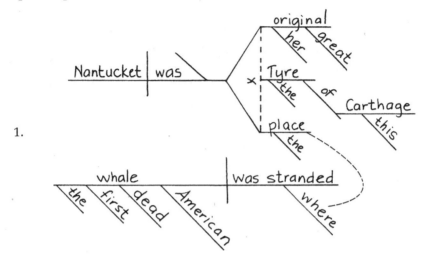

1.

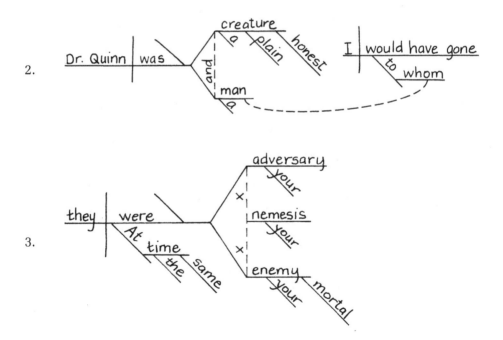

2.

3.

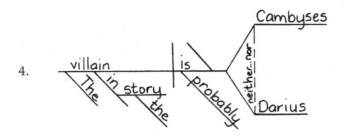

4.

3. Infinitives as predicate nominatives

1.

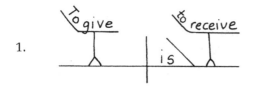

2.

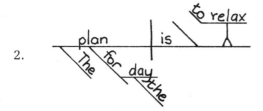

3.

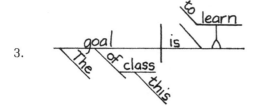

4.

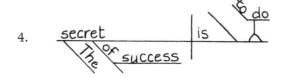

PART VI: PHRASES AND CLAUSES

VIA. Phrases

1. Verb phrases

1.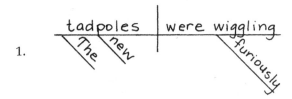

2.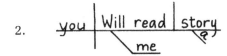

3.
```
she │Has answered
         \knowledgeably
```

4.
```
play │will end
  \the  \dramatically \Tonight
```

2. Gerunds and infinitive phrases as direct objects

1.

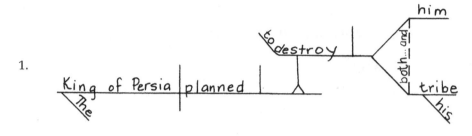

2.

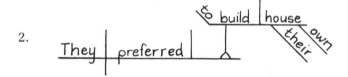

3.

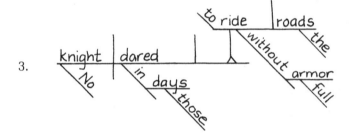

4.

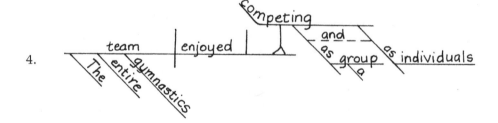

3. Gerund and infinitive phrases as subjects

1.

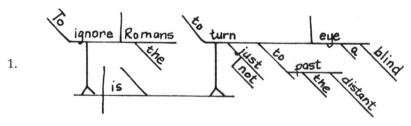

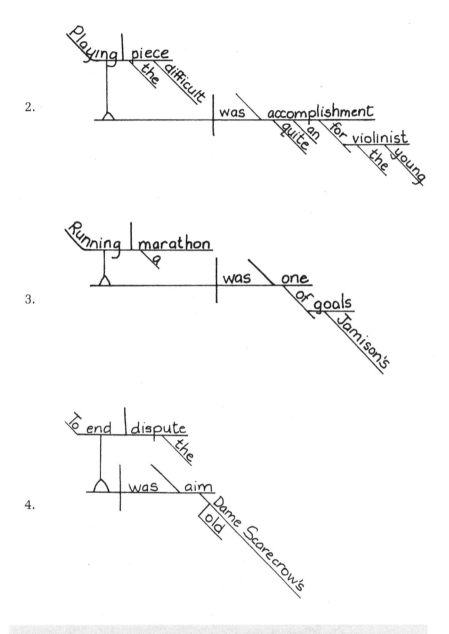

2.

3.

4.

NOTE: This is an odd occurrence of *old* acting as an adverb instead of an adjective–because it is modifying the possessive proper adjective *Dame Scarecrow's*.

4. Gerund and infinitive phrases as predicate nominatives

1.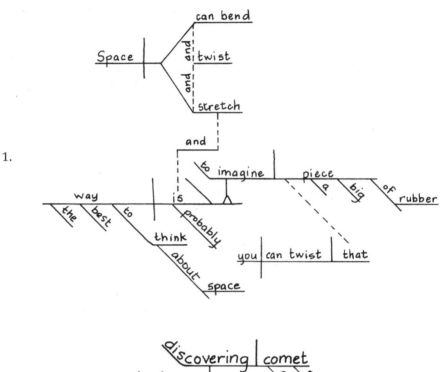

2.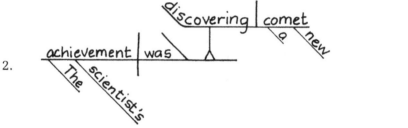

3.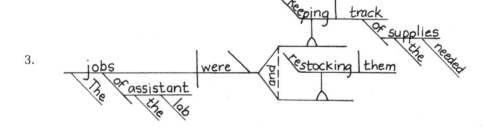

4.

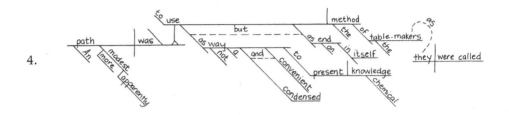

> NOTE: In the diagram, *apparently* modifies *modest*, but could also be
> diagrammed as modifying *more* (it is both *apparently more* modest, and
> more *apparently modest*).The two prepositional phrases *as a way* and *as*
> *an end* are both adverbial and modify the infinitive *to use* (which itself
> serves as the predicate nominative renaming *path*). The subordinate
> clause *as they were called* modifies the noun *table-makers*.

5. Participle and infinitive phrases as predicate adjectives

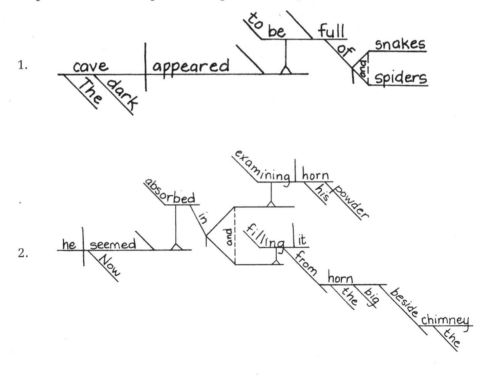

3.

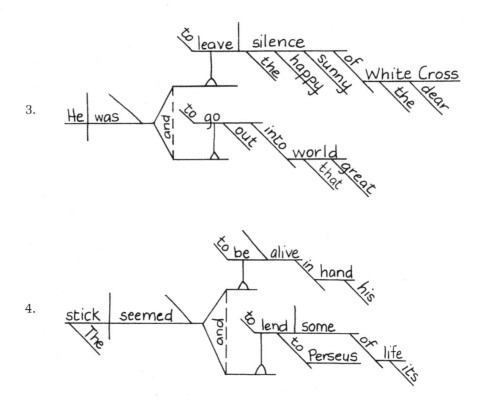

4.

NOTE: The infinitives *to be* and *to lend* both serve as predicate adjectives, following the linking verb *seemed* and describing *stick*. The adjective *alive* follows *to be* and serves as another predicate adjective, while the indefinite pronoun *some* follows *to lend* and serves as a direct object.

VIB. Independent Clauses

1. Multiple Independent Clauses

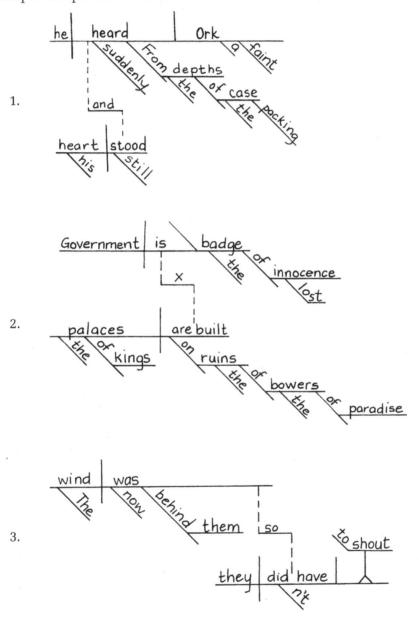

1.

2.

3.

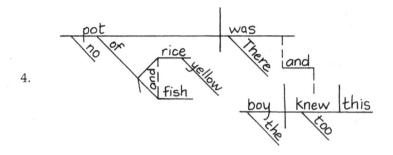

4.

VIC. Dependent Clauses

1. Dependent clauses acting as adjectives

Relative adjective examples

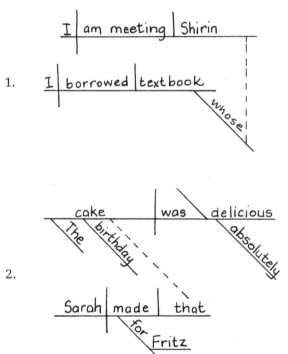

1.

2.

3.

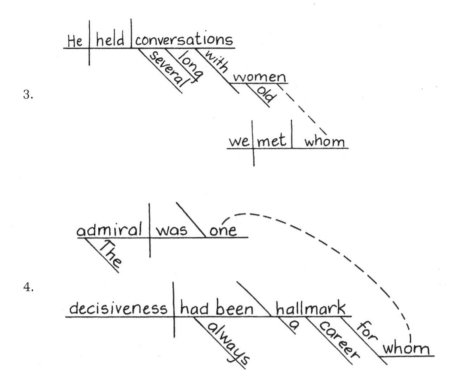

4.

Relative adverb examples

1.

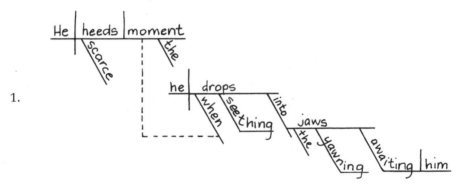

2.

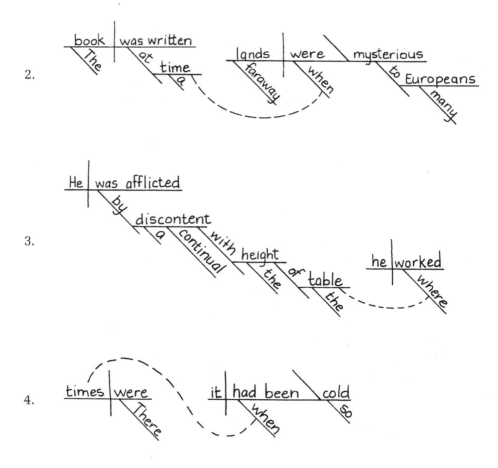

2. Dependent clauses acting as adverbs

1.

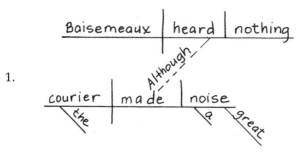

2.

3.

4.

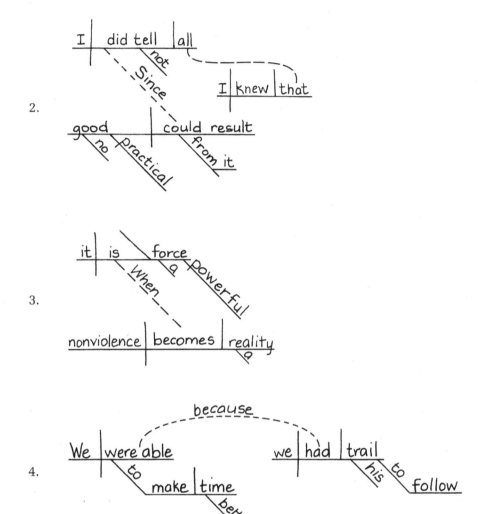

3. Dependent clauses acting as nouns

Noun clause as subject

1.
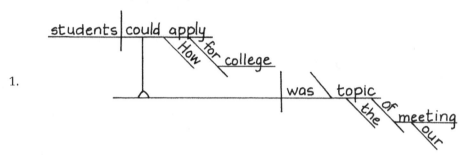

2.
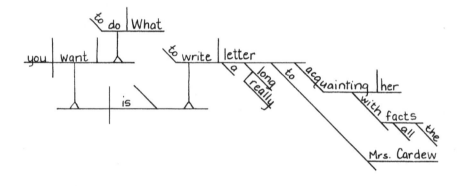

3.
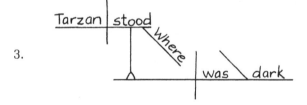

4.
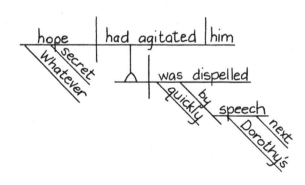

Noun clause as direct object

1.
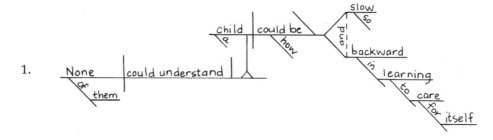

2.
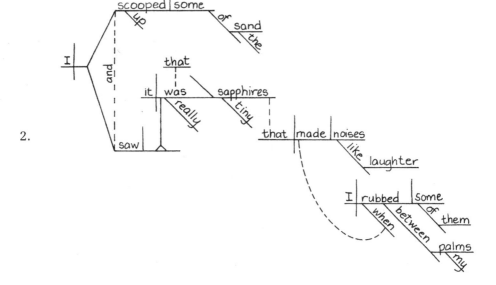

3.
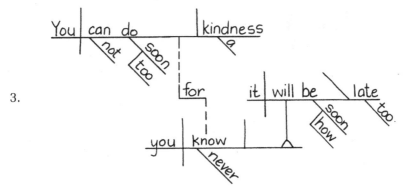

4.

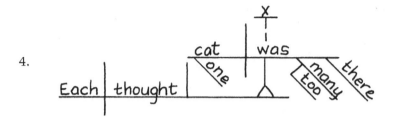

Noun clause as predicate nominative

1.

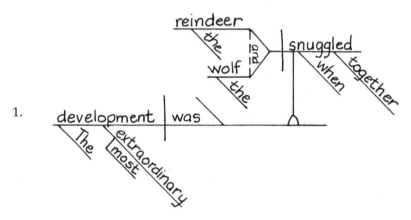

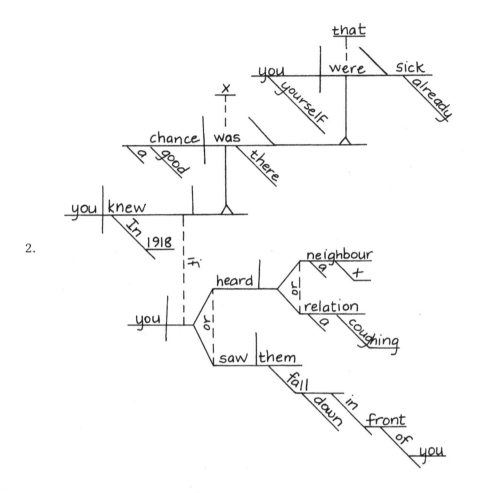

2.

NOTE: The dependent clause *[that] there was a good chance* is the direct object of the verb *knew*. The dependent clause *that you were already sick yourself* acts as a noun and is a predicate nominative renaming *chance*. The adverbial dependent clause *if you heard . . . in front of you* has a single subject and a compound verb, so the subordinating conjunction meets the predicate line before it divides. You may have trouble with the phrases *hear a neighbor or a relation coughing* and *saw them fall down in front of you*. *Coughing* is a present participle that modifies both objects of *heard*. *Them* is an object pronoun and so can't be the subject of the predicate *fall*, so *fall* must be a present participle also.

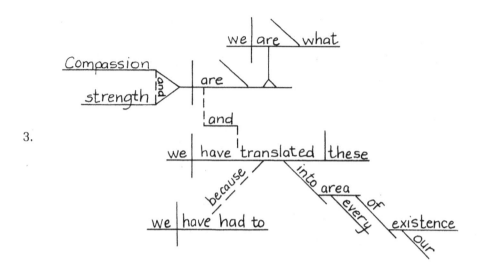

3.

NOTE: The clause *what we are* can also be diagrammed as *we are what*;
the subject and predicate nominative are interchangeable.

The verb *have had to* may be confusing; it is an idiomatic verb
bearing a single meaning, so the original diagram includes *have had to*
all on the predicate line. Alternately, *to* could be treated as the first
part of an infinitive phrase acting as the object of the verb *had*, with
understood elements: *to [translate them]*. In that case, the diagram
would appear like this:

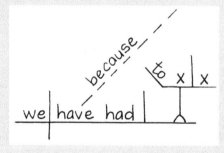

4.

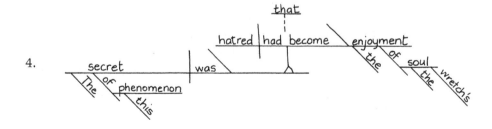

Noun clause as object of the preposition

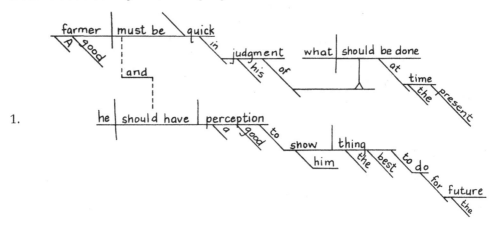

1.

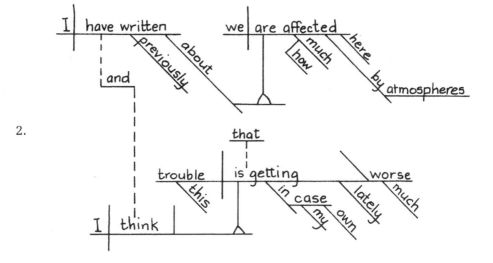

2.

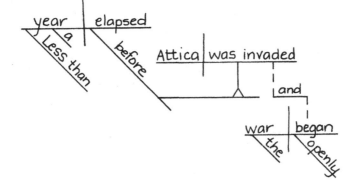

3.

4.

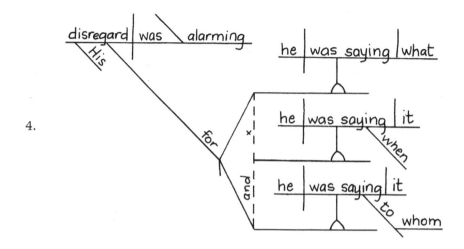

NOTE: The three clauses *what he was saying, when he was saying it, and to whom he was saying it* are all objects of the preposition *for.* It may help the student if you read her the sentence like this: *His disregard for what he was saying, [for] when he was saying it, and [for] whom he was saying it to was alarming.*

Noun clause as appositive

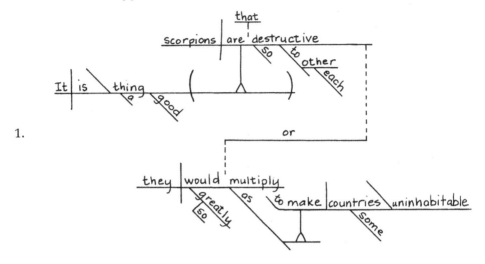

1.

NOTE: In this sentence, *uninhabitable* is an object complement describing the object *countries* and *as* serves as a preposition. The clause *that scorpions are so destructive to each other* is an appositive renaming *thing*.

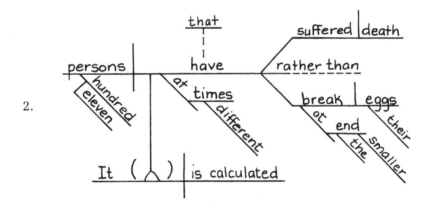

2.

Note: *Eleven hundred* can also be diagrammed on a single adjective line beneath *persons*; we have broken it into the adjective *hundred* modified by *eleven* because it is not hyphenated, but diagramming it as a single adjective is also acceptable.

3.

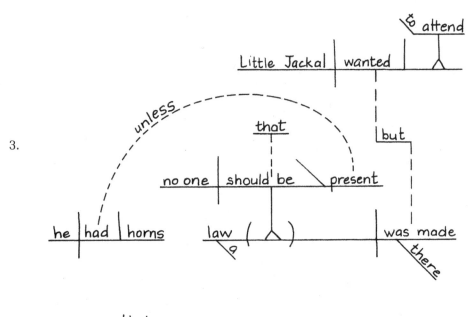

4.

Part VII: Filling up the Corners

1. Parenthetical elements

1.

Jim / and / chain / the / had / quietness / and / value

quietness / and / value

> NOTE: *Quietness* and *value* are repeated and should be diagrammed in the same way both times, but the introductory parenthetical expression doesn't have a grammatical connection to the main clause.

2.

Aunt Hester / and / went / out / once / happened / to be / absent

I / do know / not / where / or / for what

master / my / desired / presence / her / when

> NOTE: The student may have difficulty with *happened to be absent*. Although *to be absent* seems to describe *Aunt Hester*, *happened* is not a linking verb, so *to be absent* cannot be a predicate nominative. Instead, *happened* is acting as a transitive verb. In the parenthetical expression, *where* is acting as a pronoun.

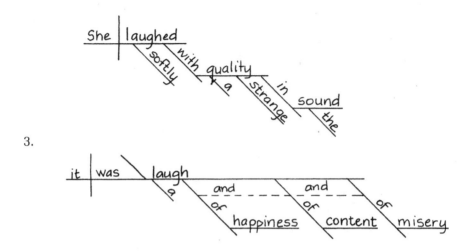

3.

NOTE: The entire expression *it was a laugh . . . of misery* is an independent element. Within that expression, *and of content* and *and of misery* both function as adjectives modifying the predicate nominative *laugh*.

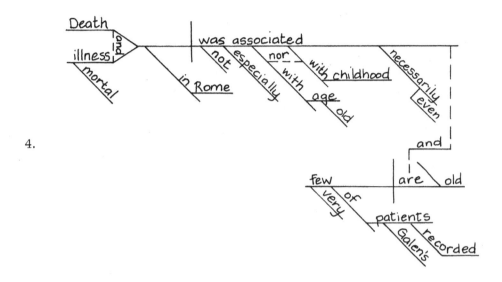

4.

NOTE: The parenthetical expression is a complete sentence that makes the original sentence compound. You may notice that the writer uses the singular verb *was* as the predicate for the compound subject *death and mortal illness*; this suggests that the writer considers *death and mortal illness* to be a single subject, but grammatically, they have to be diagrammed as two subjects. The prepositional phrase *in Rome* is probably adjectival, given its placement (*death and mortal illness in Rome*), but an argument could be made that it is adverbial and modifies *was associated* (they were associated in Rome). Because *necessarily* is an adverb, it can only modify the verb *was associated*.

2. Noun of direct address

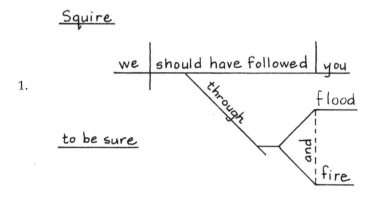

1.

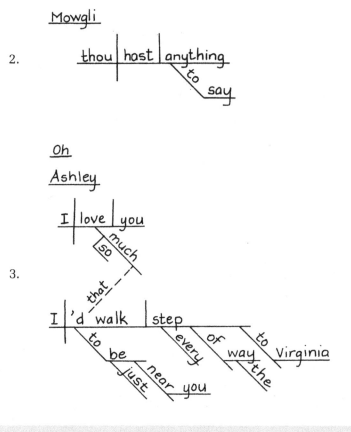

2.

NOTE: The adverb clause *that I'd walk . . . near you* modifies *much* and answers the question *how?*

4.

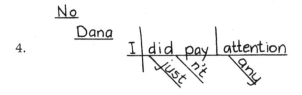

3. Interjection

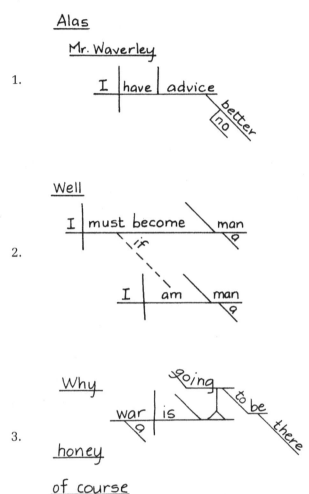

1.

2.

3.

NOTE: The phrase *going to be* can also be interpreted as an idiomatic verb, meaning that it could be placed all on the line elevated above the predicate nominative space, with *there* as an adverb modifying it. I have diagrammed both *why* and *of course* as parenthetical and below the main line, but since *why* occurs alongside the direct address term *honey*, it could also be considered an interjection.

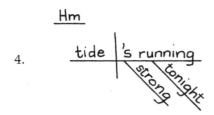

4. Phrases as appositives

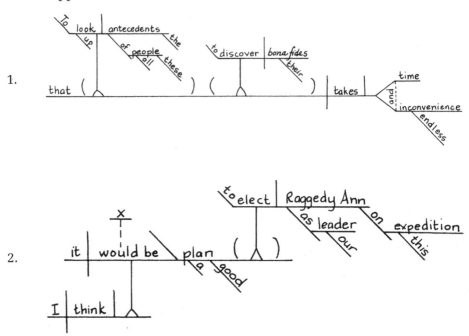

NOTE: Since the plan is *to elect Raggedy Ann*, it is diagrammed as an appositive. There is an understood "that" introducing the clause *it would be a good plan . . .*

3.

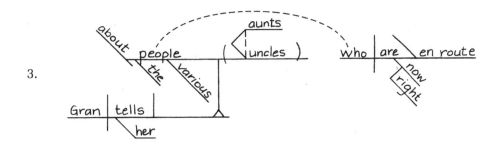

NOTE: The French phrase *en route* functions in English as a single word meaning "on the way." I have diagrammed it as a predicate adjective describing who (which people? The ones *en route*), but it could also be diagrammed as a single adverb modifying *are* (where are they? on the way). In the same vein, *now* could be diagrammed beneath the verb or beneath *en route*.

4.

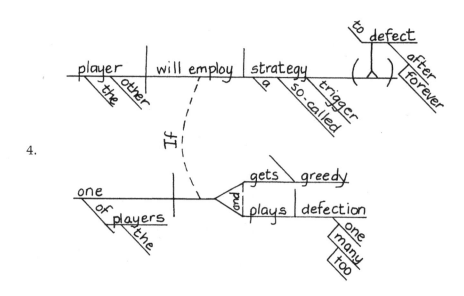

NOTE: Although this sentence has a straightforward cause/
consequence clause structure, it also has a few oddities. The infinitive
to defect is the appositive of the direct object *strategy*; *forever after* has
here been diagrammed as the adverb *after* modified by the adverb
forever, but the two words could also be diagrammed on a single
line modifying *to defect* as a compound adverb. The same is true of
the phrase *one too many*—accept any diagram that puts those three
words beneath *defection*, but show the student the diagram. This is an
idiosyncratic use of the verb *gets* as a linking verb! It is understandable
to choose to diagram *gets* as an action verb and *greedy* as an adverb,
but this diagram shows a more accurate option.

5. Absolute constructions

1.

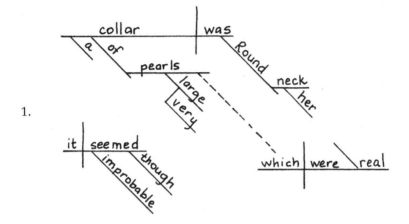

NOTE: The absolute construction is diagrammed below and to the left of the dependent clause, since it refers to the realness of the pearls rather than to the collar itself, but the placement is not vitally important. *Though* acts as an adverb within the construction. It could possibly be argued that *though* is the subordinating word connecting the adverbial clause *improbable though it seemed* to the verb *were*.

2.

3.

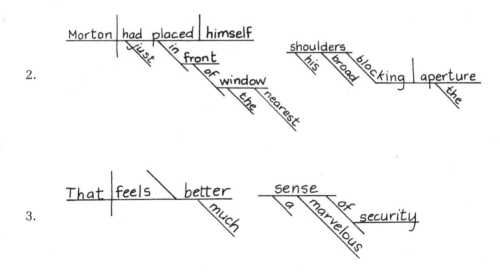

4.

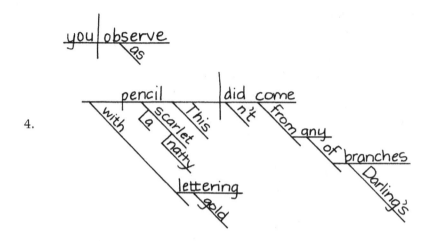

NOTE: In the absolute construction *as you observe*, the word *as* could also be diagrammed as a subordinating word. We have diagrammed it as an adverb because the clause has no grammatical connection to the rest of the sentence.

APPENDIX: CORRESPONDING LESSONS IN *GRAMMAR FOR THE WELL-TRAINED MIND*

If you are using the *Grammar for the Well-Trained Mind* curriculum along with this book, here are the lessons in that curriculum that first introduce the diagramming concepts reinforced in *How to Diagram Any Sentence.*

Part IA. Simple subjects

1. Common nouns as subjects, Lesson 10
2. The understood you as subject, Lesson 11
3. Pronouns as subjects, Lesson 11
4. Compound nouns as subjects, Lesson 25
5. Compound subjects, Lesson 26
6. Compound subjects with more than one coordinating conjunction, (not specifically taught in one lesson but demonstrated and explained in various lessons throughout the books)
7. Proper nouns as subjects, Lesson 10
8. Indefinite pronouns as subjects, Lesson 51
9. Prepositional phrases as subjects, Lesson 44
10. Demonstrative pronouns as subjects, Lesson 58
11. Interrogative pronouns as subjects, Lesson 59
12. Contractions as subjects, Lesson 36
13. Intensive pronouns with a subject, Lesson 57
14. Gerunds as subjects, Lesson 62
15. Infinitives as subjects, Lesson 63
16. Compound subjects with coordinating correlative conjunctions, Lesson 68
17. Appositive nouns after subjects, Lesson 94
18. Unknown subjects with hortative verbs, Lesson 109

Part IB. Simple predicates

1. Helping verbs, Lesson 12
2. Compound predicates, Lesson 26
3. Compound predicates with more than one coordinating conjunction (not specifically taught in one lesson but demonstrated and explained in various lessons throughout the books)
4. Contractions as predicates, Lesson 36
5. The understood helping verb, Lesson 80
6. Quasi-coordinators joining compound predicates, Lesson 105

Part IIA. Adjectives

1. Descriptive adjectives, Lesson 25
2. Compound adjectives (single adjectives made up of more than one word), Lesson 25
3. Articles, Lesson 25
4. Compound adjectives, (two or more adjectives modifying the same noun), Lesson 36
5. Possessive pronouns as adjectives, Lesson 49
6. Indefinite pronouns as adjectives, Lesson 51
7. Demonstrative pronouns as adjectives, Lesson 58
8. Interrogative pronouns as adjectives, Lesson 59
9. Past participles as adjectives, Lesson 61
10. Present participles as adjectives, Lesson 61

IIB. Adverbs

1. Adverbs that modify verbs, Lesson 33
2. Adverbs that modify adjectives, Lesson 35
3. Adverbs that modify other adverbs, Lesson 35
4. Compound adverbs (two or more adverbs modifying the same word), Lesson 36
5. Interrogative adverbs, Lesson 34
6. Adverbs of affirmation, Lesson 118
7. Adverbs of negation, Lesson 118

IIIA. Prepositional phrases acting as modifiers

1. Prepositional phrases that act as adjectives, Lesson 41
2. Prepositional phrases that act as predicate adjectives, Lesson 44

3. Prepositional phrases modifying other prepositional phrases, Lesson 44
4. Prepositional phrases that act as adverbs, Lesson 42

IIIB. Prepositional phrases acting as nouns

1. Prepositional phrases that act as subjects, Lesson 44
2. Prepositional phrases that act as direct objects, Lesson 44
3. Prepositional phrases that act as predicate nominatives, Lesson 44
4. Prepositional phrases that act as objects of the preposition, Lesson 44

IIIC. Objects of prepositions, special cases

1. Compound objects of prepositions (not specifically taught in one lesson but demonstrated and explained throughout the books, starting in Lesson 48)
2. Gerunds as objects of prepositions, Lesson 62

Part IVA. Direct Objects

1. Direct objects, Lesson 29
2. Compound direct objects, Lesson 29
3. Compound predicates with compound direct objects, Lesson 29
4. Compound predicates with the same direct object, (not specifically taught in one lesson but demonstrated and explained in various lessons throughout the books, starting in Lesson 29)
5. Interrogative pronouns as direct objects, Lesson 59
6. Demonstrative pronouns as direct objects, Lesson 58
7. Gerunds as direct objects, Lesson 62
8. Infinitives as direct objects, Lesson 63
9. Compound nouns or proper nouns as direct objects, (not specifically taught in one lesson but demonstrated and explained in various lessons throughout the books, starting with Lesson 29).
10. Understood direct object, Lesson 71
11. Appositive nouns after direct objects, Lesson 94
12. Object complements, Lesson 40

Part IVB. Indirect objects

1. Indirect objects, Lesson 37
2. Compound indirect objects, Lesson 37
3. Proper nouns as indirect objects, Lesson 37

Part VA. Predicate adjectives

1. Predicate adjectives, Lesson 38
2. Compound predicate adjectives, Lesson 38
3. Prepositional phrases as predicate adjectives, Lesson 44

Part VB. Predicate nominatives

1. Predicate nominatives, Lesson 39
2. Compound predicate nominatives, Lesson 39
3. Infinitives as predicate nominatives, Lesson 63

Part VIA. Phrases

1. Verb phrases, Lesson 12
2. Gerund, participle, and infinitive phrases as direct objects, Lesson 64
3. Gerund and infinitive phrases as subjects, Lesson 64
4. Gerund and infinitive phrases as predicate nominatives, Lesson 64
5. Participle and infinitive phrases as predicate adjectives, Lesson 64

Part VIB. Independent clauses

1. Multiple independent clauses, Lesson 79

Part VIC. Dependent clauses

1. Dependent clauses acting as adjectives, Lesson 70
2. Dependent clauses acting as adverbs, Lesson 72
3. Dependent clauses acting as nouns, Lesson 73

Part VII: Filling up the Corners

1. Parenthetical elements, Lesson 88
2. Noun of direct address, Lesson 93
3. Interjection, Lesson 93
4. Phrases as appositives, Lesson 94
5. Absolute constructions, Lesson 96

How to Diagram Any Sentence uses examples from the *Grammar for the Well-Trained Mind* series by Susan Wise Bauer.

ABOUT *GRAMMAR FOR THE WELL-TRAINED MIND*

Core Instructor Text

Scripted lessons make it possible for any parent or teacher to use the program effectively.

Step-by-step instruction takes students from the most basic concepts through advanced grammatical concepts. The *Instructor Text* is used for all four years for the *GFTWTM* series.

Student Workbooks

Each workbook allows students to practice the grammar they have learned.

Students can start with any workbook in the series, as the program is cyclical, meaning that the same concepts are covered in each workbook, but with different exercises.

Diagramming exercises reinforce the rules and help technical and visual learners to understand and use the English language effectively. Each step of the diagramming process is illustrated and thoroughly explained to the student. Examples and exercises are drawn from great works of literature, as well as from well-written nonfiction texts in science, mathematics, and the social sciences. Regular review is built into each year of work.

Purple Workbook   *Red Workbook*
Blue Workbook   *Yellow Workbook*

Keys to Student Workbooks

Each Key to the workbooks provides not only the answers, but also explanations for the parent/teacher.

Key to Purple Workbook *Key to Red Workbook*
Key to Blue Workbook   *Key to Yellow Workbook*

The Grammar Guidebook and The Diagramming Dictionary

Both are capable of accompanying the *Grammar for the Well-Trained Mind* program or standing on their own as lifelong reference companions.

The Grammar Guidebook assembles into one handy reference work all of the principles that govern the English language—from basic definitions ("A noun is the name of a person, place, thing, or idea") through advanced sentence structure analysis. Each rule is illustrated with examples drawn from great literature, along with classic and contemporary works of science, history, and mathematics.

The Diagramming Dictionary functions just like *The Grammar Guidebook*, but regarding sentence diagramming. Every rule of sentence diagramming is recorded and illustrated with easy-to-understand, color-coded diagrams—from the simplest sentences to the most complex constructions.